LOUIS BRÁILLE

GREAT ACHIEVERS

LIVES OF THE PHYSICALLY CHALLENGED

LOUIS BRAILLE

INVENTOR

Jennifer Fisher Bryant

Chelsea House Publishers

New York • Philadelphia

CHELSEA HOUSE PUBLISHERS

EDITORIAL DIRECTOR   Richard Rennert
EXECUTIVE MANAGING EDITOR   Karyn Gullen Browne
EXECUTIVE EDITOR   Sean Dolan
COPY CHIEF   Robin James
PICTURE EDITOR   Adrian G. Allen
ART DIRECTOR   Robert Mitchell
MANUFACTURING DIRECTOR   Gerald Levine
PRODUCTION COORDINATOR   Marie Claire Cebrián-Ume

GREAT ACHIEVERS: LIVES OF THE PHYSICALLY CHALLENGED

SENIOR EDITOR   Kathy Kuhtz Campbell

Staff for LOUIS BRAILLE
ASSOCIATE EDITOR   Martin Schwabacher
COPY EDITOR   Nicole Greenblatt
EDITORIAL ASSISTANT   Kelsey Goss
PICTURE RESEARCHER   Alan Gottlieb
SERIES DESIGN   Basia Niemczyc
COVER ILLUSTRATION   Alex Zwarenstein

First Printing

1   3   5   7   9   8   6   4   2

Library of Congress Cataloging-in-Publication Data

Bryant, Jennifer.
Louis Braille / Jennifer Fisher Bryant.
p. cm.—(Great achievers)
Includes bibliographical references and index.
Summary: A biography of the nineteenth-century Frenchman, accidentally blinded as
a child, who originated the raised-dot system of reading and writing used by the blind
throughout the world.
ISBN 0-7910-2077-0
      0-7910-2090-8 (pbk.)
1. Braille, Louis, 1809–1852—Juvenile literature. 2.Teachers, Blind—France—
Biography—Juvenile literature. 3. Blind—Printing and writing systems—Juvenile
literature. [1. Braille, Louis, 1809–1852. 2. Blind. 3. Teachers. 4. Physically handicapped.] I. Title. II. Series: Great achievers (Chelsea House Publishers)
HV1624.B65B79 1993   93-13025
686.2'82'092—dc20   CIP
[B]   AC

CONTENTS

A Message for Everyone   *Jerry Lewis*   7

On Facing Challenges   *John Callahan*   10

1   FRANCE HONORS ITS NATIVE SON   13

2   THE HARNESSMAKER'S SON   21

3   LEARNING TO LIVE IN DARKNESS   33

4   PARIS, THE CITY OF LIGHT   47

5   THE SEEDS OF INVENTION   63

6   TEACHER, AUTHOR, MUSICIAN   75

7   THE DIFFICULT YEARS   87

8   THE STRUGGLE ENDS   99

Further Reading   107

Chronology   108

Index   110

GREAT ACHIEVERS

LIVES OF THE PHYSICALLY CHALLENGED

JIM ABBOTT
baseball star

LUDWIG VAN BEETHOVEN
composer

LOUIS BRAILLE
inventor

CHRIS BURKE
actor

JULIUS CAESAR
Roman emperor

ROY CAMPANELLA
baseball star

RAY CHARLES
musician

ROBERT DOLE
politician

STEPHEN HAWKING
physicist

HELEN KELLER
humanitarian

JACKIE JOYNER-KERSEE
champion athlete

RON KOVIC
antiwar activist

MARIO LEMIEUX
ice hockey star

MARLEE MATLIN
actress

JOHN MILTON
poet

MARY TYLER MOORE
actress

FLANNERY O'CONNOR
author

ITZHAK PERLMAN
violinist

FRANKLIN D. ROOSEVELT
U.S. president

HENRI DE TOULOUSE-LAUTREC
artist

STEVIE WONDER
musician

A Message for Everyone

Jerry Lewis

Just 44 years ago—when I was the ripe old age of 23—an incredible stroke of fate rocketed me to overnight stardom as an entertainer. After the initial shock wore off, I began to have a very strong feeling that, in return for all life had given me, I must find a way of giving something back. At just that moment, a deeply moving experience in my personal life persuaded me to take up the leadership of a fledgling battle to defeat a then little-known group of diseases called muscular dystrophy, as well as other related neuromuscular diseases—all of which are disabling and, in the worst cases, cut life short.

In 1950, when the Muscular Dystrophy Association (MDA)—of which I am national chairman—was established, physical disability was looked on as a matter of shame. Franklin Roosevelt, who guided America through World War II from a wheelchair, and Harold Russell, the World War II hero who lost both hands in battle, then became an Academy Award–winning movie star and chairman of the President's Committee on Employment of the Handicapped, were the exceptions. One of the reasons that muscular dystrophy and related diseases were so little known was that people who had been disabled by them were hidden at home, away from the pity and discomfort with which they were generally regarded by society. As I got to know and began working with people who have disabilities, I quickly learned what a tragic mistake this perception was. And my determination to correct this terrible problem soon became as great as my commitment to see disabling neuromuscular diseases wiped from the face of the earth.

I have long wondered why it never occurs to us, as we experience the knee-jerk inclination to feel sorry for people who are physically disabled, that lives such as those led by President Roosevelt, Harold Russell, and all of the extraordinary people profiled in this Great Achievers series demonstrate unmistakably how wrong we are. Physical disability need not be something that blights life and destroys opportunity for personal fulfillment and accomplishment. On the contrary, as people such as Ray Charles, Stephen Hawking, and Ron Kovic prove, physical disability can be a spur to greatness rather than a condemnation of emptiness.

In fact, if my experience with physically disabled people can be taken as a guide, as far as accomplishment is concerned, they have a slight edge on the rest of us. The unusual challenges they face require finding greater-than-average sources of energy and determination to achieve much of what able-bodied people take for granted. Often, this ultimately translates into a lifetime of superior performance in whatever endeavor people with disabilities choose to pursue.

If you have watched my Labor Day Telethon over the years, you know exactly what I am talking about. Annually, we introduce to tens of millions of Americans people whose accomplishments would distinguish them regardless of their physical conditions—top-ranking executives, physicians, scientists, lawyers, musicians, and artists. The message I hope the audience receives is not that these extraordinary individuals have achieved what they have by overcoming a dreadful disadvantage that the rest of us are lucky not to have to endure. Rather, I hope our viewers reflect on the fact that these outstanding people have been ennobled and strengthened by the tremendous challenges they have faced.

In 1992, MDA, which has grown over the past four decades into one of the world's leading voluntary health agencies, established a personal achievement awards program to demonstrate to the nation that the distinctive qualities of people with disabilities are by no means confined to the famous. What could have been more appropriate or timely in that year of the implementation of the 1990 Americans with Disabilities Act than to take an action that could perhaps finally achieve the alteration of public perception of disability, which MDA had struggled over four decades to achieve?

On Labor Day, 1992, it was my privilege to introduce to America MDA's inaugural national personal achievement award winner, Steve Mikita, assistant attorney general of the state of Utah. Steve graduated magna cum laude from Duke University as its first wheelchair student in history and was subsequently named the outstanding young lawyer of the year by the Utah Bar Association. After he spoke on the Telethon with an eloquence that caused phones to light up from coast to coast, people asked me where he had been all this time and why they had not known of him before, so deeply impressed were they by him. I answered that he and thousands like him have been here all along. We just have not adequately *noticed* them.

It is my fervent hope that we can eliminate indifference once and for all and make it possible for all of our fellow citizens with disabilities to gain their rightfully high place in our society.

ON FACING CHALLENGES

John Callahan

I was paralyzed for life in 1972, at the age of 21. A friend and I were driving in a Volkswagen on a hot July night, when he smashed the car at full speed into a utility pole. He suffered only minor injuries. But my spinal cord was severed during the crash, leaving me without any feeling from my diaphragm downward. The only muscles I could move were some in my upper body and arms, and I could also extend my fingers. After spending a lot of time in physical therapy, it became possible for me to grasp a pen.

I've always loved to draw. When I was a kid, I made pictures of everything from Daffy Duck (one of my lifelong role models) to caricatures of my teachers and friends. I've always been a people watcher, it seems; and I've always looked at the world in a sort of skewed way. Everything I see just happens to translate immediately into humor. And so, humor has become my way of coping. As the years have gone by, I have developed a tremendous drive to express my humor by drawing cartoons.

The key to cartooning is to put a different spin on the expected, the normal. And that's one reason why many of my cartoons deal with the disabled: amputees, quadriplegics, paraplegics, the blind. The public is not used to seeing them in cartoons.

But there's another reason why my subjects are often disabled men and women. I'm sick and tired of people who presume to speak for the disabled. Call me a cripple, call me a gimp, call me paralyzed for life.

Just don't call me something I'm not. I'm not "differently abled," and my cartoons show that disabled people should not be treated any differently than anyone else.

All of the men, women, and children who are profiled in the Great Achievers series share this in common: their various handicaps have not prevented them from accomplishing great things. Their life stories are worth knowing about because they have found the strength and courage to develop their talents and to follow their dreams as fully as they can.

Whether able-bodied or disabled, a person must strive to overcome obstacles. There's nothing greater than to see a person who faces challenges and conquers them, regardless of his or her limitations.

Blind students Brian Murphy (left), age 8, and Berle Bransky, age 12, unveil a bronze bust of Louis Braille in New York City in 1952. The statue was presented to the government of France in honor of the 100th anniversary of Braille's death.

1

FRANCE HONORS
ITS NATIVE SON

ON JUNE 20, 1952, in the village of Coupvray, France, grave diggers prepared to open a grave that had remained untouched for 100 years. In it lay the body of Louis Braille, one of the world's greatest inventors and one of its most gifted geniuses.

Born in a cottage just a few hundred yards away, Louis Braille lived only 43 years. Within that short time, however, he accomplished what men for centuries before him had attempted in vain: he developed a revolutionary system of reading and writing for the blind.

"In the whole history of communication, there have been only a few cases in which an inspired individual has brought about sweeping change," wrote Braille biographer Gary Webster. Braille's invention, he argued, compares favorably with "Gutenberg's printing press, Bell's telephone, and Edison's phonograph [which] have affected the course of civilization."

On that misty summer morning in 1952, Braille's body was gently and respectfully removed from its resting place and transferred to a padded double coffin. His hands, which had transformed his dreams and ideas into a revolutionary language for the blind, were preserved as relics in the village where he was born nearly a century and a half earlier.

The following morning, blind delegates from 40 countries came to the graveyard for a memorial service. They stood solemnly around the coffin of the man who, through years of hard work, sacrifice, and personal suffering, had single-handedly opened the door of knowledge for blind men and women everywhere.

As the ceremony drew to a close, they prepared to accompany Braille's coffin on the 25-mile trip to Paris, where he would be taken to his final resting place. Passing through the village square—renamed La Place Braille, or Louis Braille Square, in honor of its most famous citizen—members of the delegation paused to run their hands over the smooth bronze statue that had been erected there in 1887. "A Braille Les Aveugles Reconnaissants" (To Braille, The Grateful Blind) read the inscription on the

In June 1952, blind delegates from 40 countries gathered for a ceremony at Louis Braille's grave site in his hometown of Coupvray, France. Braille's body was exhumed and carried to Paris, where it was laid to rest in the Pantheon, the burial place of France's most honored citizens.

stone base. On the top rested a bronze likeness of Braille teaching a young blind student how to read. In his lap was a book printed in the dot alphabet that he invented at the age of 15.

The procession of delegates escorted the coffin to the outskirts of Coupvray. Leaving the boundaries of his home village for the last time, Braille's body was transported over country roads to the capital. There, a week-long celebration in his honor was reaching its climax, with numerous events taking place all over the city. At the great Gothic cathedral of Notre Dame, Archbishop Feltin led a commemorative Mass. At the Sorbonne, France's most noted university, reporters for *Time* magazine covered a memorial service at which there were "more than one hundred blind delegates from twenty-two countries." Noted author and handicapped-rights advocate Helen Keller addressed the delegation: "We the blind are as indebted to Louis Braille as mankind is to Gutenberg," she said. "The raised letters under our fingers are precious pods from which has sprouted our intellectual wealth. Without a dot system, what a chaotic, inadequate affair our education would be!"

As the delegation from Coupvray was making its way to Paris, hundreds of blind people from around the world were gathering at the National Institute for Blind Youth, the school where Louis Braille himself had spent the greater part of his life. The streets of Paris between Boulevard des Invalides and Rue Soufflot, where the Pantheon—the final resting place of the greatest men and women of France—was located, were lined with curious faces.

As the warm sun cast its afternoon shadow on the "city of light," the carriage carrying Braille's coffin rolled slowly through the streets. Behind the carriage walked thousands of blind people, young and old, rich and poor, tapping their white canes on the pavement in front of them.

Blind students from France's National Institute for Blind Youth, the school where Louis Braille studied and later taught, join a procession accompanying Braille's coffin as it is carried to the Pantheon. The president of France, Vincent Auriol, was among the coffin bearers.

"The blind all over the world revere [Braille] as a genius and as their special saint," wrote Helga Lende of the American Foundation for the Blind in that week's issue of the *Library Journal.*

The coffin was removed from the carriage and carried between two rows of National Guardsmen dressed in dazzling red, black, and white uniforms. The bearers, led by French president Vincent Auriol, paused briefly as they reached the top of the stairs. Reporters snapped photographs of the group standing beneath the inscription over the doorway: "Aux grands hommes la patrie reconnaissante"—"To its great ones, the country gives honor." Inside the building, a place was being prepared for Braille's body alongside some of the most significant writers, artists, inventors, and politicians of modern times. Names such as Voltaire, Jean-Jacques Rousseau, Emile Zola, and Jean Moulin were etched in stone inside the domed, Roman-style building. According to French tradition, burial in the Pantheon is "the highest honor France can bestow."

As in the case of many of those buried in the Pantheon, the seeds of greatness were planted early in Braille's life.

The intellectual and spiritual endurance required for his achievements were rooted primarily in the steady flow of affection and encouragement he received from his family. At age three, when a terrible accident in his father's harness shop left him permanently blind, Braille's parents rose to the challenge of raising their disabled son with uncompromising courage. This was no small feat in the 19th century, for, as Helen Keller wrote in *Science Digest,* those with physical disabilities were "avoided and treated as victims of divine wrath."

Despite the ignorance of the times, Braille's parents raised Louis with the same dignity and respect they had given their three older children. He attended school, completed chores in the farmyard, harvested grapes in the vineyards, and danced at Coupvray's festivals and holiday celebrations. As a result of being treated as much like a sighted child as possible, Braille learned to experience life to its fullest, to appreciate his talents, and to develop his intellect.

As he grew older, the affection of his parents and siblings and the interest of a kindly village priest helped to strengthen his trust in people and his faith in God's will. These two characteristics would serve him well in the years ahead when frustration and despair threatened to destroy his normally cheerful disposition.

At the age of 10, Braille was accepted to the Royal Institute for Blind Youth in Paris. It was here that he formed lasting friendships and developed his exceptional musical and intellectual gifts. It was at the Institute that he was first introduced to a military captain's coded writing system that would be the basis for his own invention of a raised-dot alphabet for the blind.

Over the years, biographers and historians have pointed out the almost miraculous circumstances of Braille's invention. In retrospect, the obstacles he faced—politically, socially, and psychologically—seem overwhelming. Yet, at the age of only 15, the blond, curly-haired youth suc-

As part of a week-long celebration accompanying Braille's reburial in the Pantheon, noted American author and activist Helen Keller explains the braille alphabet in a speech at the Sorbonne, France's most illustrious university, on June 23, 1952.

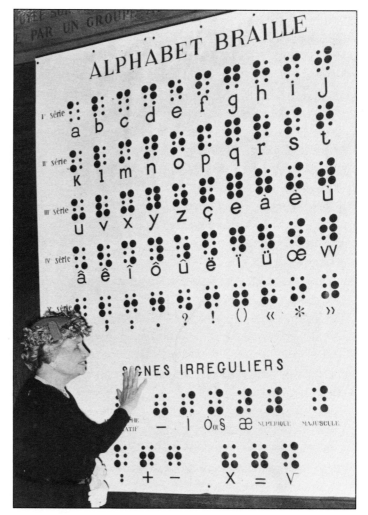

ceeded in developing a system of reading and writing for the blind that is still used today.

Like many geniuses whose ideas and contributions are rejected by their contemporaries, Braille died unaware of his success. It was not until two years after his death that "braille" (as people then began calling his system) was given official approval by the French government. Another quarter-century passed before braille was promoted throughout the rest of Europe. The United States did not adopt the system until 1917 and even then continued to experiment with different versions of Braille's basic dot alphabet. Finally, in 1949, the United Nations Education, Scientific and Cultural Organization (UNESCO) established a standard version that could be used by all languages. As of that year, more than 100 languages and as many dialects could be translated into braille.

Today, braille is used by millions of blind people around the world. Modern technology has made it possible for the rapid conversion of books and other printed material into the raised-dot alphabet. Computers have been developed that "read" printed pages and reproduce them with a braille printer. Personal computers can now be equipped with braille keyboards and monitors that allow blind students and employees to write, edit, and save material with the same speed and efficiency as their sighted counterparts.

Over the years, braille has undergone revisions and modifications, but the basic system invented in 1824 remains largely intact. Without the brilliance and sacrifice of a precocious young Frenchman, it is possible that the visually impaired might never have gained the intellectual independence they enjoy today. In the words of Helen Keller: "Were it not for the braille method of reading and writing, the world of the blind would be quite drab—worse than for the seeing without inkprint books. . . . Without braille . . . wisdom would indeed be shut out."

Louis Braille was born on January 4, 1809, in the village of Coupvray, about 25 miles east of Paris, France. Though he moved to Paris at the age of 10, he returned home to visit his family regularly throughout his life.

2

THE
HARNESSMAKER'S
SON

ON THE MORNING OF January 4, 1809, a stiff wind blew over the narrow, cobblestone streets of Coupvray, France, some 25 miles east of Paris. Like many of the inhabitants of the tiny farming village, Simon-René Braille and his family remained indoors, closing their shutters and stoking the fire against the bitter cold outside. It was especially important on this day to keep the tiny farmhouse warm and free of drafts.

Upstairs, in the small bedroom above the kitchen, Simon-René's wife lay in bed recovering from a long and exhausting night of childbirth. Monique Braille was a small woman with long, graying hair and lively eyes that made her appear younger than her 41 years. There had been talk in the village that Madame Braille would not be strong enough to bear a healthy child at her age. But earlier that morning she had proved them wrong. In her arms, she cradled her fourth child, the Brailles' second son, whom they had named Louis (pronounced "Loo-wee" in French).

It was several hours before Simon-René allowed the three older children (16-year-old Catherine-Joséphine, 14-year-old Louis-Simon, and 11-year-old Marie-Céline) to visit their mother and new baby brother. It was another full day before he took Louis to be registered at the mayor's office on the village square. The clerk's eyebrows lifted in surprise when he saw that the last Braille child had been

Braille's birth certificate records the "Naissance de Louis Braille" (Birth of Louis Braille). The fourth child of Monique and Simon-René Braille, Louis had two sisters and a brother, all of whom were more than 10 years older than he.

registered more than a decade before. "This one shall be
the companion of my old age," explained 44-year-old
Simon-René.

The baptismal service followed four days later. Because
the infant mortality rate was high in those days, it was
customary to arrange for this religious ritual quite early in
the child's life. "In Braille's own family," noted Braille
biographer Jean Roblin, "there had been a number of these
early deaths and as practicing Christians they were not

prepared to risk delay." The baptism was performed by the local parish priest and witnessed by Louis's godparents who lived on a neighboring farm.

All through that winter, Monique kept the baby well fed and warm, wrapping him snugly in a down comforter. In the course of the next two years, the scrawny, red-faced infant became a curious toddler with blond, curly hair and clear, blue eyes. With a loving mother and three eager siblings, Louis never lacked for attention—there was always someone to play with. His older brother and sisters took turns telling him stories, playing hide-and-seek, and carrying him through town on their shoulders.

When his siblings were occupied elsewhere, Louis played happily with his wooden blocks on the stone floor of the kitchen while his mother cooked, swept, and cleaned the house. With its thick walls, small windows, and moss-covered roof, the Braille home resembled many of the others that lined the streets of Coupvray. Heavy oak doors and shutters—designed to keep out the summer heat and winter cold—also kept out much of the light so that the interior was dark even on the sunniest days. To lessen this effect, Monique whitewashed the walls as often as possible and left the doors and windows open when the weather permitted. She kept a heavy black pot filled with onion soup hanging over the fire that blazed in the hearth. The smell of the simmering soup, mingled with the scent of his mother's freshly baked bread and the tangy local cheese, permeated the house.

Water for cooking, cleaning, and bathing had to be carried in wooden buckets up the stone path from the well on the lower end of the seven-acre property. Louis knew this path well and would often follow his sister Catherine when she fetched the water for a new batch of soup. Sometimes she would let him grab on to her skirts as she balanced a bucket carefully on each arm, making the task seem more of a game than a chore.

This house in Coupvray, France, now a museum, was Louis Braille's childhood home. The Brailles grew most of their own food on their seven-acre property, and the cozy house was usually filled with the smell of hot onion soup or freshly baked bread.

Each member of the Braille family had responsibilities on the small farm. Catherine was in charge of the large vegetable garden and saw to it that the planting, hoeing, weeding, and picking was done on a daily basis. Marie-Céline fed the ducks and the chickens and collected their eggs. Louis-Simon fed and groomed the horse and kept its stall clean and dry. Sometimes he would hoist his baby brother up onto the back of the milking cow as he led her to the stream to drink. Louis helped out wherever he could—shelling beans, collecting eggs, setting the table for dinner. Repeating these small but necessary chores gave him the opportunity to contribute to the family and taught him, at an early age, the value and satisfaction of productive work.

The Brailles were not a wealthy family, but their few animals, large garden, and well-tended vineyard provided them with nearly all of the food they needed. Most of the villagers lived in this way, making their living by farming or from a trade closely associated with it. Besides the full-time farmers who tended the surrounding grainfields and vineyards, Coupvray boasted a blacksmith, a wheelwright, several carpenters, a rope maker, a locksmith, a tailor, and a weaver. These were all men, as the women in these times were relegated to the more traditional tasks of keeping house and raising children.

For all of Coupvray's citizens—men, women, and children—life in the village was tied to the rhythm of the seasons. Spring was a time for tilling the soil, planting seeds, and tending to newborn livestock. Summer was spent working in the fields and fattening animals for slaughter. Autumn brought the grain and grape harvests and a week-long celebration with plenty of singing, dancing, and wine drinking. Winter was a time of recovery from nine months of physical labor. It was the time, too, when the closely knit community cared for those among them who were needy—the elderly, the sick, and the poor.

This pattern of life had not changed significantly since Louis's grandfather had come to Coupvray more than 70 years before. Attracted by the lively village on the hillside overlooking the Marne River, he had settled there in 1740, married the saddler's daughter, and later inherited his workshop. The business itself had been established in the 1600s and was passed down through the generations. By the mid-1700s, it was known throughout the local countryside for its fine harnesses and saddles produced by the skilled hands of master craftsmen.

Simon-René had taken over his father's business in 1782. Like the other village tradesmen, he had spent several years as his father's apprentice before being approved by the village trade guild. Exactly one year after acquiring the status of master craftsman, he married Monique Barron, a farm girl from a neighboring village. When Simon-René's father died he left his seven acres, small farmhouse, and adjacent workshop to the young couple and their growing family.

Like his father, Simon-René was known for his fairness and craftsmanship and had a reputation for being the finest harnessmaker in the province. His customers came to Coupvray from all corners of Île-de-France, a region which included dozens of towns, villages, and several hundred square miles of countryside around Paris. "There is Coupvray's future harnessmaker," they would say when they saw Louis playing on the floor next to the workbench. But to their surprise, Simon-René would shake his head. "Not this one," he would reply. "This one, we have decided, shall study books."

The statement might have seemed optimistic to some. But those in the Braille family knew already that Louis had a quick mind and an insatiable desire to learn. He had been a curious infant, remaining alert in his cradle for most of the day as the family moved about the house and farmyard. He had learned to talk at an earlier age than any of his siblings, and once he had mastered speech there was no end to the questions he would ask.

As Louis became older and more independent, he spent more time in the workshop watching his father fashion fine saddles and harnesses for his many loyal customers. He loved the smell of newly tanned hides and the feel of the leather when it was rubbed smooth with an oily cloth. For hours Louis would sit and watch his father—hunched over his workbench and wearing his big leather apron—create sturdy saddles, delicate reins, and intricate harnesses from the finest pieces of leather available. He watched him select the strongest pieces for girths and stirrup leathers and dye small strips of weaker pieces for decorative harness fringes.

The rows of tools hanging over the workbench fascinated young Louis more than anything else. In the skilled hands of his father, they must have seemed like the magical ingredients that made it possible for all of the shapeless leather pieces to assume their final useful form. There were sharp, pointed awls for punching holes, dull mallets for fastening rivets and buckles, and sharp knives for cutting pieces from the fat rolls of freshly oiled leather stacked in the corner. Sometimes Louis reached for a tool that Simon-René had laid aside on his workbench. "Non, non!" warned his father firmly. The sharp tools belonged only in the hands of a practiced craftsman and could never be used as playthings. To appease Louis's curiosity, Simon-René gave him scraps of leather to make into boats, horses, or toy soldiers. Louis contented himself with these, arranging the pieces into different patterns while sitting on the front step of the workshop. From there, he could safely observe the townsfolk as they went about their daily activities.

On Thursdays, he would be on the step a bit earlier than usual. Thursday was market day, and people from many of the surrounding towns and villages brought their fruits, vegetables, grains, and animals to trade in Coupvray's town square. They arrived in ox-drawn carts, on horse-back, or on foot, wearing their most colorful clothes and balancing baskets on their heads.

As the carts rolled slowly by, their thick wooden wheels bouncing over the cobbled street in front of him, Louis smiled and waved. Sometimes his mother and sisters, dressed in gaily colored skirts, took him to the square to watch the trading. On the way home, they would chatter happily as they strolled down Touarte Street, enjoying the fresh *petit-pains* (small, hard rolls) they had bought for a treat.

But in the warm days of 1812, their conversations became less cheerful. It was rumored that Emperor Napoléon Bonaparte was gathering the French army at the Rhine River, preparing the troops to march against the Russians. The outcome would not be known for several months, but talk of war was deeply disturbing to the peaceful families of Coupvray. Several times that spring, Louis heard his father whispering to the neighbors as he attempted to piece together bits of information given to him by some of his more distant customers.

It was on one such day that Louis sat near the doorway listening as his father spoke to a customer outside. Weary of playing with the leather pieces on the step, he wandered inside and climbed up on the workbench. A wide strip of leather was stretched across the surface and next to it lay one of his father's punching tools—a pointed, metal awl. Though he had been forbidden on several occasions to

As a child, Louis Braille spent many hours in the workshop of his father, a harnessmaker. It was in this workshop that Louis injured his eye with an awl at the age of three.

handle the tool, Louis's curiosity would not allow him to resist the opportunity to see what it was like. He picked up the sharp instrument and began to poke at the leather as he had watched his father do hundreds of times before. But his small, chubby hands were no match for the tough material, and instead of passing through to the other side, the awl slipped from Louis's grasp and plunged into his left eye.

His terrified scream brought both parents running immediately to his side. As his mother held him closely and tried to soothe him, his father inspected the wound. He found a clean cloth and held it over the eye, which was spurting bright red blood. In those days, there were no antiseptics available for cleansing wounds, nor were there antibiotics for preventing infection. In the early 1800s, before these germ-killing products were discovered, common illnesses and bodily injuries were routinely treated with homemade remedies. These were usually made by combining extracts from local herbs, flowers, and trees.

Louis's injury was no exception. A village woman was called in to administer a poultice soaked in a special herbal liquid. She instructed his parents to apply a clean bandage and to change the dressing several times each day.

Despite the woman's good intentions, however, the wound was too deep for such a superficial treatment. Monique changed the bandage frequently and tried to keep the bewildered child from rubbing his face, but it was no use. Infection rapidly set in and the eye became red and swollen.

There are some accounts that claim that a few days later, the Brailles consulted a doctor some 20 miles away. Other records contradict this, however. Most of the doctors at that time had been called away to serve Napoléon's troops several hundred miles to the east. It is unlikely, therefore, that Louis was ever seen by anyone with any formal medical training.

Even if Louis had been taken to a doctor, the prognosis would have surely been grim. Without antibiotics, it would have been extremely difficult to prevent an infection in a deep puncture wound such as the one Louis had received. As is evidenced by the passage below, taken from a 19th-century physician's manual, almost nothing was known about the workings of the healthy eye and even less about how to treat an injured one.

> Light should be prevented from entering the room, and the eye should be covered with compresses soaked in cold water. Bleeding of the arm, application of leeches around the injured eye, diet and a dose of calomel are the methods usually employed.

In the weeks following the accident, Louis became more uncomfortable and his parents grew more and more worried. Try as they might, they could not prevent him from scratching at the infected wound and spreading the germs to his right eye. To the family's horror, the uninjured eye became inflamed as well, and his vision became increasingly blurred. "When will morning come?" Louis asked repeatedly. Each time he asked, the family realized that the chances for Louis's recovery were growing slimmer.

By autumn of that same year, it was clear to Monique and Simon-René that their young, blond-haired son would never see again. As he sat by the hearth day after day waiting for the light to return, his family looked helplessly on and wondered what the future would hold for Louis Braille.

An illustration from "A Compendium of Medicine and Surgery" dating back to the 17th century shows an oculist receiving his patients. Before the existence of antibiotics such as penicillin, most eye diseases were incurable. Louis Braille's own blindness resulted from an infection spreading from his injured eye to his healthy eye.

3

LEARNING TO LIVE IN DARKNESS

THE BRAILLE FAMILY'S FEARS were not unfounded. In the early 19th century, people with significant physical handicaps—including blindness—were not considered part of normal society. They were treated as outcasts and were often subjected to physical and emotional abuse.

The history of such cruelties began hundreds of years earlier. In Roman times, for example, groups of blind people were kept as slaves by sighted owners who trained them to sit on street corners and moan loudly and pitifully. Passersby occasionally dropped a few coins in their laps, and these small earnings went immediately into the pockets of their abusive owners. The enslaved beggars were barely clothed and poorly fed and were beaten severely or abandoned if they rebelled.

In the Middle Ages there was some improvement. Monasteries and convents opened their doors to the blind, offering them food and shelter in exchange for simple housekeeping duties. Although this was a more pleasant alternative to begging, churches could not employ more than a few at a time. In those days, blind beggars roamed the streets living on what they could find in garbage heaps or outside the doorways of compassionate citizens. These vagabonds were frequently hit, tripped, kicked, and spat upon by sighted people in whose view they were filthy nuisances with no rights of their own. As Braille biographer Anne Niemark explains in her book *Touch of Light*:

> The blind had stumbled through history on a lonely and terrifying road. Many had been locked away in mental institutions, or used as freak attractions, or simply left to wander in the streets. The world of instruction and learning—of books and schools—had been shut off from them. In fact, to be blind meant to be helpless and unschooled and forever dependent on someone else.

At the time of Louis's injury, Coupvray had its own blind beggar who had wandered into town one day from the Paris highway. Memories of this man, dressed in rags and stumbling along the narrow streets, haunted Louis's parents. After the initial shock of the accident had passed and they knew that their son's blindness was permanent, they resolved never to allow Louis to end up in such a state. Somehow, they would help him attain a degree of self-sufficiency and independence normally reserved for the sighted.

To encourage this, however, they would have to treat him as normally as possible, resisting the temptation to overprotect him because of his blindness. Watching him make mistakes and endure the inevitable frustration that would accompany his new situation would be difficult. But for Louis's sake, they decided, it must be done.

Throughout the winter and into the spring of the following year, Louis began the process of readjustment. It was exhausting at first, and he felt as if he were a baby learning to walk all over again. His knees and shins became sore from bumping into the low, wooden benches at the kitchen table and tripping over the heavy rug that lay in front of the hearth. Recalling how easily he used to move around the house and the farmyard, he sometimes yelled in frustration at his clumsiness. When he and Catherine went to collect the eggs, he stumbled repeatedly on the stone path leading to the henhouse. Monique stood at the back door and watched, offering words of encouragement when Louis returned, crying and bruised, with his basket of broken eggs.

Gradually, however, Louis began to use his other senses to compensate for his loss of sight. His father made him a wooden cane that he tapped in front of him as he walked around the property. He found that if he hummed or sang as he went, he could use the echo from his voice to sense walls or large objects in his path. He memorized the number of paces it took him to cross each room of the house, how many from the front door to his father's workshop, from the workshop to the neighbor's house, and so on.

His sense of smell, he discovered, served him nearly as well as his sense of touch. He learned to distinguish the aroma of his mother's onion soup from that of the neighbors'. He located the bakery by following the scent of fresh dough, and the stable by its smell of hay and horses.

From his favorite perch on the front step of the workshop, he trained his ears to do the work his eyes had once done. Though the village bustled with activity, especially on market day, Louis found that he could easily identify the many different voices, footsteps, and vehicles on the street below. The quick clip-clop of horses' hooves meant that a stage was passing through; a slow, plodding gait was a farmer's oxen team pulling a heavy load. A fast group of individually mounted horses meant that soldiers had arrived. When people passed on foot, he listened for a distinguishing trait: the swish of a wealthy woman's

Though it was not luxurious, the Braille home, with its whitewashed walls and stone floors, was comfortable enough for Louis's family. But when the Brailles were forced to provide first for Napoléon's retreating Grand French Army, and then the victorious Russian troops that occupied the village, the family's resources were stretched to the limit.

skirt, the stomping of a soldier's boots, the jingling pocket change of the baker, the cough of the blacksmith.

With each passing day, Louis stored more of these impressions in his memory. He became bolder, surprising friends and neighbors by calling out to them as they passed by. Happy to see that he was not becoming helpless and withdrawn, they responded, "Bonjour, Louis! Ça va?" (Hello, Louis! How are you?)

As Louis's confidence increased, the mood of the Braille household lifted. By the time they celebrated his fifth birthday in January 1814, Monique and Simon-René felt they had much to be thankful for. They began to set aside some money for Louis's future, hoping that a small inheritance, combined with his quick mind and cheerful disposition, would be enough to sustain his independence when they were gone.

In the months that followed, however, this sense of hope and security rapidly diminished. Word reached Coupvray that Napoléon's Grand French Army had been defeated at the Rhine River and was falling back toward Paris. Couriers were dispatched to the towns east of the city with orders to furnish the retreating soldiers with food and supplies. In Coupvray, the mayor called a town meeting on the square and read the emperor's request out loud. The news was not good. The citizens of Coupvray were expected to give 400 bushels of oats, 1,200 bales of hay, 700 loaves of bread, and 12 cows and horses.

The war-weary villagers had no choice but to fill the order. Reluctantly, the Brailles gave their cow and their horse to the army, and the surplus from the vegetable garden was allotted to the hungry troops. They rationed carefully what little was left and waited for spring to arrive.

But as the days grew longer and warmer, the situation did not improve. Napoléon's reckless attempt to dominate all of Europe and Russia left his empire in a shambles. He was forced to abdicate and Louis XVIII became the new king of France. The French soldiers, routed by the Russians, were driven back to Paris. The foreign troops then occupied villages in the path of the army's retreat and forced the inhabitants to shelter and feed them. Coupvray was one such village.

The occupation placed a new set of demands on Louis who, though adjusting remarkably well, was still learning how to get around on his own. During the two years of

The grand ambitions of Emperor Napoléon I (1769–1821) to conquer all of Europe and Russia cast a shadow of war over Louis Braille's childhood.

enemy occupation the Brailles had little time to spare for Louis's special needs. They focused instead on producing enough food to feed themselves and the soldiers who billeted with them.

Rather than risk an unfriendly confrontation with the Russians stationed on the streets, Louis stayed close to home. He passed the hours sitting by the fireplace, braiding

Starving French soldiers retreat from Moscow after a disastrous attempt by Napoléon's army to conquer Russia. The retreating troops stayed for a while in Coupvray, followed by the Russians, who had vanquished and then pursued them.

tassels for harnesses or arranging scraps of leather into different shapes and patterns. His father made him a toy dog that he held closely to his chest whenever the soldiers came stomping into his mother's kitchen, demanding a hot meal.

The tensions of the house were somewhat relieved by visits to his father's workshop. The smell of the tanned

hides, the feel of soft strips of leather, and the familiar sounds of his father punching and pounding at the workbench were a source of comfort to Louis at a time when all else around him seemed threatening. But the workshop was less busy than it had been before the war. Now there were few customers, and Simon-René occupied himself with repairing saddles, bridles, and harnesses for the Russian troops. Without a steady income, he was forced to use the money he had set aside for Louis to feed and clothe the family.

In the spring of 1815, a glimmer of hope pierced the gloomy atmosphere of the village. A young priest named Jacques Palluy was appointed to the local parish. During the first months of his ministry, Palluy made a point of visiting each and every home in Coupvray. Louis was immediately drawn to the kind young man, and the priest reciprocated his affection. Observing how eagerly Louis followed the adults' conversations and how quickly he responded to his own polite questions, Palluy concluded that a keen intelligence lay behind the boy's sightless stare.

During one of his visits, Palluy asked for permission to tutor Louis three times a week at the parish. When he promised to instruct him in practical matters as well as religious ones, the Brailles agreed.

The hours spent with Abbé Palluy were some of the best of Louis's young life. Sitting under the trees in the churchyard or inside the presbytery nearby, the Abbé told Louis stories from the Bible and read him short works of literature and poetry. He taught him about the movement of the stars, the changing patterns of weather, and the habits of common animals. Louis listened intently to the priest's every word, feeding his imagination with images from the past and present. He memorized the names of famous writers and artists and recited long verses of poetry. He followed Palluy on walks around the garden, learning to distinguish flowers by their scents and textures, and to identify birds by their chirps and songs. He developed a

Jacques Palluy, a young priest appointed to Louis's parish in 1815, took an interest in the six-year-old boy and offered to tutor him. Louis eagerly listened as Palluy taught him about religion, literature, and natural science. Louis's intelligence so impressed the priest that he persuaded the village schoolmaster to admit Louis to the village school.

profound religious faith that, though initially concentrated on Bible stories and children's songs, was to continue to evolve throughout his lifetime.

The lessons at the church continued for more than a year. Louis proved to be a natural student whose intellectual curiosity was enthusiastically nurtured by the scholarly priest. It fascinated Louis that one man could have such an endless store of knowledge. But Palluy knew that there was much more to learning than stories and poetry, and he began to wonder if Louis should spend more time with children his own age.

When Louis questioned his teacher about the village school, Palluy knew it was time for Louis to move on. He approached the village schoolmaster, a young man named

Antoine Becheret, and asked if Louis might be admitted. Because of the special circumstances, Becheret wanted some time to consider the request.

Fortunately, the cards were stacked in Louis's favor. His parents were hard-working, respected citizens well known for their kindness and generosity. Most of the villagers had known Louis before the accident and were not opposed to his attending school with their own sighted children. The fact that Palluy had initiated the request made Becheret's decision somewhat easier than it might otherwise have been. Because the Abbé held the respect and admiration of nearly everyone in Coupvray, his recommendation carried a great deal of influence. And so, at the risk of displeasing education authorities in Paris (who might not permit a blind child to be educated with sighted children), Becheret gave his approval.

Each morning, beginning that same week, one of the boys from the school met Louis at the front door of the Braille cottage. Together, they walked the steep slope of Touarte Street to the schoolhouse where Louis proudly took his place in the front row of wooden benches. Leaning forward, his head tilted slightly sideways, he learned to sit quietly and listen during lectures and to respond clearly and quickly to the questions that followed. Louis understood the risk that Becheret had taken in admitting him to the school and promised himself that the schoolmaster would never regret his decision.

Within weeks, Louis's natural intelligence asserted itself and he excelled in nearly every subject. His superb memory, which had served him well during his lessons with Palluy, now became his biggest asset. He could recite the history lesson, delivered orally by Becheret the previous day, almost flawlessly. Equally adept at arithmetic, he calculated difficult problems in his head long before the other students arrived at the answer on paper.

Yet, for all his intelligence, there was no provision for a blind boy in Coupvray to learn reading and writing.

When the other students took out their primers and slates, Louis could only sit quietly and listen to the rustling of pages and the scratching of chalk. He reluctantly settled for asking his sister Marie or one of his classmates to read to him after school.

But for Louis, who had been encouraged since the accident to be as independent as possible, this was not an acceptable arrangement. "Are there no books for blind boys to read?" he asked Becheret repeatedly. The young schoolmaster was forced to tell Louis the truth. "None that I know of," he would answer sympathetically. Then he reminded Louis how much he had learned despite the fact that there was nothing for him to read.

Louis turned to his family for support. One account tells how Simon-René hammered round-topped upholstery nails into a board so that Louis might learn the alphabet. Using his fingers, Louis practiced tracing the outline of each letter, saying each one out loud. In a similar fashion, his sister Catherine taught Louis how to form words from letters made of straw. The two of them would sit on the kitchen floor and send messages to each other, Louis giggling in delight at his newfound talent. This kind of encouragement later contributed to Louis's persistence in creating his own system of reading and writing. Had he been raised in less fortunate circumstances—in a family which equated physical disabilities with stupidity, for instance—his story would have surely ended differently.

For the next three years, from eight o'clock in the morning until five o'clock at night—with a short break for lunch—Louis attended the village school. He never took his education for granted, but instead tried each day to learn as much as he could. At the end of each year, it was not unusual for Louis to finish the year at the top of his class. His parents, never boastful, were nonetheless proud of their son's achievements. The Abbé was equally delighted with the progress of his young protégé and resolved to find a way for Louis to continue his education.

After several months of looking into the matter, the Abbé devised a plan which he presented to Monique and Simon-René. He told them of a special school for the blind in Paris where Louis could further develop his talents. There, the priest explained, he would learn a trade, play an instrument, and even read books that were printed using a special method.

Louis's parents received the news somewhat stoically, certain that the cost of the school would be prohibitive for peasants such as themselves. Palluy had anticipated their reaction, however, and offered to ask the local estate owner

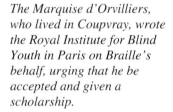

The Marquise d'Orvilliers, who lived in Coupvray, wrote the Royal Institute for Blind Youth in Paris on Braille's behalf, urging that he be accepted and given a scholarship.

for her assistance. He felt sure that if the Marquise d'Orvilliers wrote to the Paris school on Louis's behalf, he would be able to obtain a scholarship.

Though it was clear that Louis would gain some advantages by attending the Royal Institute for Blind Youth in Paris, the Brailles hesitated in giving their consent. Instead, they asked for some time to think the matter over.

For the next several nights, after the children had gone upstairs to bed, Monique and Simon-René weighed the various factors in their decision. They wondered who would take care of Louis if he was ill or lonely or lost. Perhaps a boy of 14 or 15 would be ready to leave home and live in the city for nine months each year, but surely at age 10 Louis was too young and too naive for such a drastic change.

In the end, however, it was Louis who helped them decide. When he heard that there were books that blind people could read, he pleaded with his parents to let him go to the school in Paris. Reluctantly, the Brailles gave Palluy their permission to pursue his plan.

By the end of January 1819, the Brailles received a letter from the Royal Institute for Blind Youth announcing Louis's acceptance and offering him a scholarship. With mixed emotions, the family helped Louis prepare to leave home for the first time. He would be back, they knew, but for the most part his fate now lay in the hands of a few men in Paris whose faces they had never seen. The night before Louis was to leave, his family gathered in front of the fireplace and prayed for his safety and for the kindness and wisdom of those in whose care Louis would now be placed.

François Lesueur, a former beggar, was the first blind student taught by pioneering educator Valentin Haüy. Haüy fed and clothed the blind boy and taught him manners, grammar, and arithmetic. Lesueur's achievements helped Haüy win the financial backing he needed to open the first school for blind youth in Paris, which Louis Braille attended 35 years later.

4

PARIS,
THE CITY OF LIGHT

WHEN LOUIS BRAILLE entered the Royal Institute for Blind Youth in 1819, the school was already 35 years old. It had been founded by Valentin Haüy who, at age 26, had witnessed a spectacle that would forever change his life. At the Fair of St. Ovid in 1771, Haüy had stood among the crowd watching a group of blind musicians perform. But the exhibition was not the serious one that Haüy had expected. The musicians wore huge cardboard "eyeglasses" and dunce's hats with donkey's ears taped to the sides. Their musical scores were set in front of them upside down, and they banged, strummed, and plucked randomly on worn-out wooden instruments.

Haüy was outraged at the audience's inhumanity as the crowd laughed hysterically at the mockery onstage. He felt there was no justification for treating people in such a cruel manner simply because they were blind. From that day on, he committed himself to bettering the plight of blind people.

Being both an intelligent and compassionate man, Haüy believed that the visually impaired deserved an alternative to a life of begging and freak shows: they deserved an education. And so, several years later, he convinced a 17-year-old blind beggar named François Lesueur to become his first pupil. With his own money, Haüy fed, clothed, and took care of Lesueur and began teaching him manners, grammar, and basic arithmetic. He taught Lesueur the alphabet using a set of movable wooden

At the Fair of St. Ovid in 1771, a crowd gathered to mock a group of blind people dressed in ridiculous costumes who were made to perform in a clownish concert. Valentin Haüy was so appalled by the degrading spectacle that he devoted the rest of his life to providing educational opportunities for the blind.

letters and showed him how to form words by arranging the letters inside a wooden frame.

By accident, Haüy discovered that Lesueur could feel raised printing on the reverse side of pages from some of his own books. Building on this idea, Haüy embossed several pages himself by pushing the outline of large letters into heavy sheets of waxed paper. He then glued the sheets together to form a single double-sided page and taught Lesueur to read them by touch.

The innovative teacher and his eager pupil presented their achievements to the French Academy, which included the nation's foremost scholars. When the Academy offered Haüy its support, he opened the world's first school for blind children in Paris. Two years later, students from the school gave a demonstration of reading and arithmetic for King Louis XVI at the court of Versailles. The king was impressed and gave Haüy the financial backing he needed to hire more teachers and to expand the curriculum.

In 1791, after the king had been overthrown by French revolutionaries, the Royal Institute for Blind Youth came under the jurisdiction of the new French government. But when Napoléon came to power eight years later, he immediately ordered the school to merge with an asylum for the elderly blind known as l'Hôpital des Quinze-Vingts. When Haüy realized that there would be no real education offered for the blind under the new regime, he protested vehemently. He was subsequently fired and, fearing for his safety, he fled to Russia. There, the idea that blind people could be educated was still a novelty, and according to biographer Gary Webster, people "shook their heads in disbelief that children they had thought mentally retarded by blindness actually could learn." Nonetheless, Haüy managed to gain the support of Czar Alexander I and founded a second school for the blind.

After Napoléon's abdication in 1814, the Paris school was allowed once again to function on its own, and Dr.

Valentin Haüy helped create the possibility of an education and a dignified existence for blind children in France. His appeals to the French Academy and King Louis XVI and his convincing evidence that the blind could be educated led to the creation of the Royal Institute for Blind Youth in Paris.

Sebastien Guillié was hired to direct it. Haüy was denied the opportunity to visit, however, because Guillié considered his protests during the revolution treasonous. Enrollment grew steadily throughout the early 1800s, and by 1819, when Louis Braille set off for Paris to attend the Institute, there were 60 full-time students.

As he sat quietly next to his father and felt the stage bounce and sway over the frozen dirt highway, Louis tried to sort out the thoughts and feelings that were swirling around inside of him. Ever since he had received the letter

announcing his acceptance to the Institute he had anticipated this day. He had lain awake many nights trying to
imagine what life at the Paris school would be like.

But now that the day had arrived, he felt a mixture of
delight and apprehension. Saying good-bye to his mother,
brother, and sisters at the town square had been difficult
enough. As the carriage had rolled away and the familiar
sounds and smells of the village grew distant, Louis began
to feel true loneliness for the first time in his life. He kept
up a lively conversation with his father to hide his anxiety.

Simon-René was struggling with feelings of guilt and
doubt, and as the carriage rolled through the frost-covered
countryside, he played along with Louis's charade.
Though he believed that his son deserved an opportunity
to be fully educated, he worried about leaving him in the
immense and crowded city, a place so very different from
the quiet community of Coupvray.

The journey took nearly four hours. It was early afternoon when the stage pulled to a stop at the City Gate. After
paying the driver, Louis and his father walked through the
crowded streets of Paris, crossing the Seine River on a
footbridge to arrive on the Left Bank. Like all of the city's
academic institutions, the Royal Institute for Blind Youth
was located in a section known as the Latin Quarter. (In
earlier times, Latin was the official language of scholars.)
As they made their way slowly through the neighborhood,
Louis used his other senses to try to form a picture of the
city. He was overwhelmed by the number of unfamiliar
sounds and smells that surrounded him, however, and
decided to leave that task for the future.

It was late in the afternoon when Louis and his father
arrived at 68 Rue St. Victor. Simon-René was shocked by
the dilapidated condition of the four-story stone building
and was glad that Louis could not see his trembling hand
knocking on the heavy wooden door. A caretaker answered and led them down a dark, narrow hallway. As they
followed him, Simon-René observed the damp-smelling,

poorly lit classrooms, broken windows, and well-worn stairways. Suppressing his anxiety, he squeezed his son's hand reassuringly and, forcing a smile onto his face, entered the director's office.

Smiling broadly himself, Dr. Guillié invited Louis and his father to sit in the two chairs facing his desk. He shook Simon-René's hand and welcomed Louis to the school, informing him that he was the youngest student enrolled. Patiently, he answered Simon-René's questions about the methods of instruction and the daily routine. He assured him that Louis would be well cared for and that, with the help of a sighted assistant, he would regularly send letters home.

The director's confidence alleviated many of Simon-René's fears. A practical man, he reasoned that the opportunity for Louis to attain an advanced education outweighed the possible disadvantages of living in an old, run-down building. Outside the director's office, he gave Louis a final hug and told him to do his best and to write his mother often.

His father turned to go and Louis listened as the footsteps grew fainter. When the front door of the school slammed shut, he was truly alone for the first time in his young life. Briefly, he considered running after his father and begging him to take him home to Coupvray. But, like Simon-René, Louis had learned not to act on impulse. "He had a fertile imagination but it was always controlled by reason," Dr. André Pignier would later write.

Fortunately, there was not much time to think about being afraid and lonely. Dr. Guillié hurried Louis up the stairs and down the hall to the classroom where Monsieur Dufau's geography lesson was in progress. The other blind students immediately stood when the director entered the room, pushing Louis ahead of him. But Guillié's mood had shifted since the friendly chat with Simon-René. Commanding the boys to remain seated so that the lesson could continue, he brought Louis to an empty seat and told him to remain there until the end of class.

Louis tried his best to focus on the lesson, but the excitement of traveling and being in the city left him little energy for concentration. Feeling slightly bewildered, he listened as M. Dufau lectured on the history of the Seine River and its importance to French agriculture. When he had finished, Dufau fired questions at each of the students. Finally, he came to Louis. Louis answered nervously, anxious to make a good first impression. Dufau, who carefully guarded his authority in the classroom, grunted his approval.

After dismissing the class, Dufau assigned an older student to be Louis's guide. The guide escorted him to the dormitory, which Louis discovered consisted of a large room with two long rows of cots on either side. He followed his guide to his assigned cot and put his few belongings underneath. His mother had packed him a box full of special pastries and a whole chicken that she had cooked for him the night before. This, too, Louis pushed under his cot before setting off to explore the school building with his guide.

After a brief tour of the classrooms and a bland but warm meal of rice and beans in the cafeteria, Louis returned to the dormitory. Feeling tired and already a bit homesick, he reached underneath his bed, but found nothing. The boy in the next bed listened as Louis groped in vain for his mother's care package. "That's just the way it is here," he said quietly.

The boy was 11-year-old Gabriel Gauthier. He remembered how it had felt to be the newest student and tried to save Louis additional disappointment. After introducing himself, he explained the common practice of "hazing" that the older students inflicted upon the newer ones. There would be a few more weeks of nasty tricks, practical jokes—and yes, even stealing, Gauthier assured him.

The two boys stayed awake for several hours, Louis telling Gauthier about his family and Gauthier telling Louis about the school. The next day he talked to Louis between classes and sat with him at meals. At the end of the first week, Louis dictated a letter to his mother telling her that his bed was cold and hard, the food was poor, but he had at least made a good friend.

It took several more weeks for Louis to find his way independently around the school and to feel comfortable with the routine. The narrow corridors and worn, twisting stairways would have been a challenge even for a sighted child. Though he could not see its condition, Louis sensed that the building was in drastic need of repair. The light was dim and the circulation poor, creating a damp, unhealthy atmosphere. Several of the older students had chronic coughs and it was rumored that government officials had threatened to close the facility unless improvements were made. Alphonse de Lamartine, a renowned poet and historian, said in his report to the Chamber of Deputies:

> No description could give you a true idea of this building, which is small, dirty and gloomy . . . of those many tortuous, worm-eaten stairways which [are] far from suited to unfortunates who can guide themselves only by their sense of touch.

There was only one bathroom, so the students were allowed to bathe just once each month. Having grown accustomed to the fresh air and clean smells of the countryside, Louis was disgusted by the foul smells that seemed to invade every corner of the building. It was because of this, Louis learned, that visitors brought scented cloths to hold over their noses while touring the facility.

Like the building itself, members of the school's staff were cold and unfriendly. Gauthier had warned Louis in advance of Guillié's temper and Dufau's strict code of classroom behavior. Even a slight infraction of the rules would result in a student being denied a day's meals or

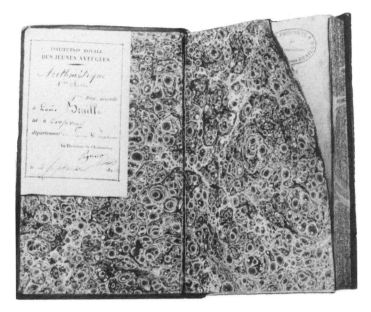

This book, which belonged to Louis Braille, bears a label awarding Louis the first prize for arithmetic in his class. Although Louis was the youngest student in the school when he entered, his keen intelligence and hard work made him a top student by the end of his first year.

being placed in solitary confinement. Armed with this knowledge, Louis was careful never to appear disrespectful and to follow the school's policies as closely as possible. The rules seemed harsh, especially compared to the friendliness he had known from Palluy and Becheret.

Nevertheless, Louis understood that this school—for better or for worse—was his only chance to secure a productive future. Each day he put on his uniform—black wool trousers and waistcoat trimmed in gold with brass buttons—and hurried to the cafeteria for a light breakfast of rolls and milk. Classes in history, grammar, math, and Latin followed, during which students sat passively at their desks as their sighted teachers gave lengthy lectures. The students were then asked to recite portions of the lesson or to answer specific questions about it. Louis had hoped for a more sophisticated style of teaching, and he was disappointed to learn that the approach was the same as it had been in Coupvray.

After morning classes, there was time for a break outside in the courtyard. Because the classroom atmosphere was so strict, it was only during this recess that Louis allowed his good-natured playfulness to surface. The boys (girls were not yet admitted to the Royal Institute for Blind Youth) organized relay races and games of leapfrog and a modified version of "tag." Students who preferred less physical pursuits could play checkers or chess on specially designed boards.

Afternoon was always easier than the morning, with only geography and music lessons remaining. Louis was a gifted musician, with an excellent ear, quick hands, and strong, nimble fingers. He studied the cello and organ and in a short time could play complicated pieces on both instruments.

In addition to his musical training and academic work, Louis was assigned to work several hours each week in the

The students at the Royal Institute for Blind Youth spent several hours a week in the school workshop making slippers and purses that were sold to provide funding for the school, as this picture from a book by Professor Guillié of the Institute illustrates. Young Louis, whose nimble fingers were accustomed to such chores from spending hours in his father's harness workshop, won a prize for the quality of his handiwork in the factory.

slipper factory. The factory workshop was run by the school, and its profits were used to pay salaries and to defray the cost of supplies. Doing handiwork reminded Louis of the days he had spent in his father's harness shop. Often, he found himself thinking about home as he sewed the leather pieces together and passed them down the line.

By the time spring arrived, Louis's initial shyness had disappeared and he had grown more confident. As he became more assertive, his intellectual gifts became more apparent, and his teachers took notice. One, Dr. André Pignier, described Louis as "possessed of a lively intelligence" and called his oral reports "models of exact thinking, remarkable for their precision of thought and for the clarity and correct language in which it was expressed." By the end of the first year, Louis was at or near the top of his class in every subject. In addition, he was given the top prize for his handiwork at the slipper factory.

And yet, in spite of this success, Louis was restless and frustrated. He had come to the Institute, in large part, to learn to read. Thus far, however, he had been given no opportunity to do so. While classroom lectures honed Louis's superb memory, they did nothing to increase his intellectual independence. He soon realized that unless he learned to read and write on his own, his scope of knowledge would be forever limited to what he was taught by his sighted teachers.

Louis began making regular requests to visit the school's library. But when his requests were repeatedly denied, he grew angry and confused. He could not understand why the school bothered having books if the students were not given free access to them. Finally, his friend Gauthier told him the truth. The "library," he explained, consisted of only three books and a few pamphlets that were stored in a back room. The books were large, clumsy, and very expensive to print. Some of the older students knew how to read them but even they were only occasionally given the opportunity to do so. "There are other things for you to do besides read books," Guillié would say.

Louis was devastated. He had imagined a large room filled from floor to ceiling with books printed especially for the blind. And, given the fact that only a few really existed, he was not willing to wait much longer to have a try at reading them. Perhaps, Louis thought, his teachers might give him a chance sooner if he continued to do well in his classes.

His suspicion was confirmed at the beginning of his second year when M. Dufau announced that Louis would be taught to read the school's few "big books." Louis could hardly contain his excitement—this was the chance he had been waiting for.

When the day finally arrived, a servant carried two of the volumes—a French grammar book and a copy of the morning and evening prayer—into the classroom. An older student showed Louis how to begin by tracing the outline of the large letters with his fingertips. Holding Louis's hand in his own, he moved it slowly across the page from left to right. Immediately Louis was reminded of the leather and straw letters he had played with on the floor of his father's workshop.

The older student helped him through the first few pages, then allowed him to do the next few on his own. But as Louis neared the end of the book, his enthusiasm waned. The reading process was slow, and even with his excellent memory he often forgot the first letters of a sentence by the time he got to the end. He was then obliged to return to the beginning and start over. Because each sentence took up more than a page, the book contained no more than a few paragraphs.

To Louis, who was very practical, this seemed horribly inefficient, and he concluded that far too much effort was required to access such a tiny amount of information. The

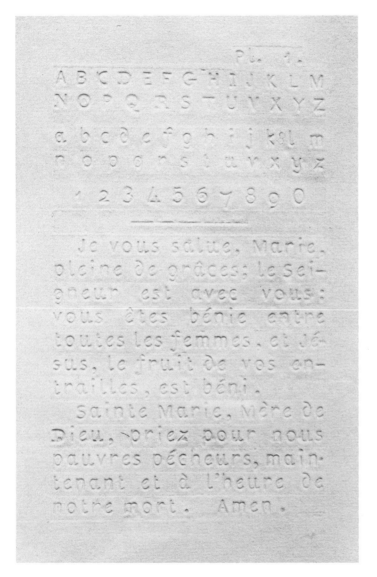

Before the invention of Braille's raised-dot alphabet, the only books that the blind could read were printed with a system of large, embossed letters that was developed by Valentin Haüy. The shapes of the letters were laboriously pressed into waxed paper.

more he read the books, the more he felt as if he were being teased. The few prayers and basic grammar concepts that the books contained were not nearly enough—he wanted to know much more. He longed for a better method, one that was less cumbersome and more practical than Haüy's embossed letters.

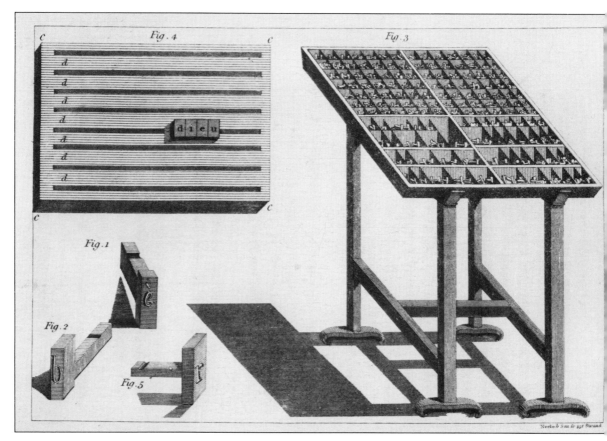

This illustration from Guillié's book shows how raised letters were affixed to a frame so that their shapes could be pressed into pages that the blind could read.

Louis began to ask questions about the other methods of reading and writing that had been created. Perhaps, he thought, a system could be developed that would offer the blind a greater opportunity for communication and expression. Through his teachers, he learned that inventors were always bringing their ideas for new methods of touch-reading to the Institute. Occasionally, the students had been permitted to try them in the classroom: letters carved in wood, knots tied into long pieces of rope, even pins nailed into a board.

Each of these methods, however, had proved to be impractical and incomplete. Though slow and expensive, Haüy's method of embossed letters on waxed pages was the only one still in use, the only one comprehensive

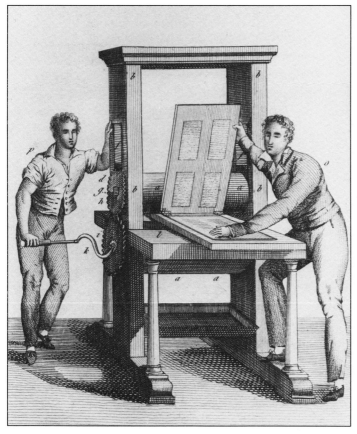

Another illustration from Guillié's book shows two men preparing to press pages of type into a sheet of paper, leaving an imprint that could be felt with the fingertips.

enough to allow for the production of books. And so, as biographer Gary Webster observed, "There was little real reading at the famous Institute. . . . The great world of books remained behind a door that was, for all practical purposes, still closed to the blind."

Captain Charles Barbier, who served for several years in the Signal Corps of King Louis XVIII's army, invented a code system called nightwriting that allowed soldiers to send and read messages in the dark. Barbier's system of raised dots and dashes provided the original basis for the idea later refined and developed by Louis Braille.

5

THE SEEDS OF INVENTION

IMPORTANT DEVELOPMENTS in the year 1821 later proved to have great influence on the life and work of Louis Braille. At the beginning of his third year at the Institute, the board of directors announced that Dr. Guillié was being released from his duties. An investigation had confirmed rumors that Guillié had developed "an intimate relationship with the schoolmistress," and the board immediately hired Dr. Pignier to replace him.

The new director was a more lenient and sensitive man who, to the delight of the students, suggested that the school's harsh rules be relaxed. The atmosphere of the school remained formal, but punishments were less severe. When they *were* handed out, it was in the interest of improving a student's behavior and not simply as an assertion of the teacher's authority.

Pignier treated the students with respect and encouraged them to achieve academically. He made a habit of visiting the classrooms so that he could to get to know each pupil personally. In his diary, he recorded his impressions of many of them, including that of Louis Braille.

> [He has] a certain childish gravity . . . well-suited to the delicacy of his features and the gentleness and intelligence of his expression.

In the spirit of reform, Pignier invited Valentin Haüy to return to the school that Haüy had founded nearly 40 years before. He felt it was appropriate to publicly honor Haüy's accomplishments and to give the students an opportunity to meet the man who was responsible for their educational opportunities. After receiving Haüy's affirmative reply, the students began planning a day-long celebration that would include games, music, poetry, craft displays, and a reading demonstration.

On a hot summer day in 1821, parents, friends, students, and faculty gathered in the school's courtyard to pay tribute to Valentin Haüy. The chorus sang, the band played, and a few students read selections from the embossed books. Louis was one of the readers and, though anxious, received thunderous applause for his flawless performance. Dr. Pignier gave a speech in which he thanked Haüy for being "a brave pioneer" in the cause of educating the blind.

After the ceremony was over, visitors toured the building, nodding approvingly at the decorated hallways and classrooms. A reception was held in the largest room to allow teachers, parents, and students to visit informally. To those who had known the school under Guillié's administration, it was clear that things had changed for the better.

Finally, it was time for the students to shake hands with M. Haüy and offer him a few words of thanks for his many years of hard work and dedication. When it was Louis's

After Valentin Haüy protested the poor treatment of his school by Emperor Napoléon, he was forced to flee to Russia, where he established another school for the blind. Even after Napoléon's abdication in 1814, Haüy was still considered a traitor and was forbidden to visit the school he had created. In 1821, he was finally welcomed back to the school with an official ceremony. He met and shook hands with several students, including Louis Braille.

turn, he approached the old man nervously. But Haüy greeted him warmly, gently clasping Louis's pudgy young hands with his own frail, bony ones. Later, Louis would recall that moment as a high point in his life—a moment of true inspiration. It seemed as if some great force of energy, some inexplicable understanding was communicated in that brief exchange between the elderly founder

and the 12-year-old boy from Coupvray. In the future—
during periods of frustration, ill-health, and despair—the
memory of Haüy's warmth and sincerity would help Louis
persevere through difficulties.

He would picture Haüy gathering the students around
him at the end of the celebration and proclaiming "through
tears of gratitude" that "It is God who has done everything."

While the spiritual motivation for Louis's future invention was provided by a man of education—Valentin
Haüy—the practical basis for the breakthrough was provided by a man of the military—Charles Barbier. A retired
artillery captain who had served in Louis XVIII's army,
Barbier had been assigned for several years to the Signal
Corps. One of his duties there was to establish an effective
means of battlefield communication.

He had developed a method of "nightwriting," a code
system that allowed French soldiers to send messages back
and forth in the dark without betraying their position to the
enemy. Different combinations of dots and dashes were
punched into heavy paper using a sharp, pointed tool called
a stylus. Each combination represented a common sound,
and groups of combinations stood for words and phrases.
By positioning a multi-grooved ruler underneath a sheet
of paper, a commander could punch out brief orders such
as "The enemy is advancing," "Fall back," or "Be ready to
march at dawn."

In 1821, Barbier called on the chairman of the Royal
Institute for Blind Youth's board of directors to demonstrate a modified version of nightwriting. He believed that
the new version, which he called sonography, might be
useful as a system of reading and writing for the blind. Like
nightwriting, sonography was a phonetic language in
which a series of dots and dashes were punched into paper
with a stylus. The resulting raised imprints were then read
with the fingertips on the reverse side of the page.

The chairman was sufficiently impressed by Barbier's system to suggest that he meet with Dr. Pignier. Encouraged by the chairman's opinion, Barbier went home to prepare a presentation for the director.

Pignier received the news with a mixture of excitement and skepticism. Over the years, many inventors had come to the school claiming to have discovered a revolutionary method of reading and writing. But so far none of the new methods had lasted. The chairman's enthusiasm was not enough to convince Pignier that Barbier's sonography would be any different and he remained doubtful.

During the meeting, however, Pignier became more optimistic. After witnessing Barbier's carefully organized demonstration and having a try at the system himself, the director concluded that sonography could be used as an alternative method at the Institute. He agreed to present the system to the staff and the students, suggesting that it be employed at once in the classroom.

This diagram demonstrates sonography, the code of raised dots and dashes invented by Charles Barbier. Sonography used large groups of dots to denote various sounds. Braille reduced the number of dots and used them to represent letters of the alphabet, making the system more efficient and versatile.

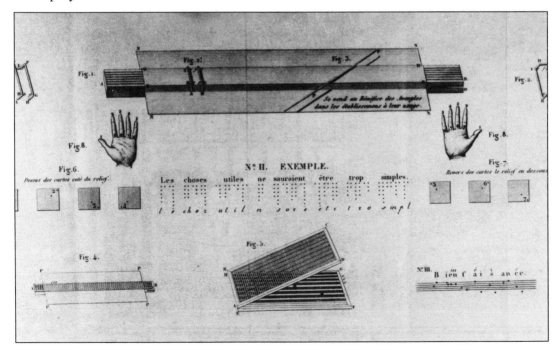

A few days later, the students gathered together in the school's dimly lit auditorium and listened as Pignier explained the basic concepts of sonography. Louis and Gauthier sat among the others, whispering excitedly as they fingered the paper, stylus, and slate that were being passed around the room. The chatter became louder as several examples of messages written in the embossed code were provided and the students were shown how to "read" the messages with their fingertips.

Louis was astonished. Unlike the big, clumsy letters of the library books, the dots and dashes of sonography were remarkably easy to feel. In addition, there was the incredible advantage of being able to write.

For Louis, who had always valued independence and self-expression, sonography was a real breakthrough. His sharp, curious mind seized upon the new method and he began at once to memorize its symbols. Together with Gauthier, Louis volunteered to practice writing a few messages. Positioning the stylus carefully in the grooves of the slate, they punched slowly and awkwardly at the heavy paper. Soon, however, they were able to accurately copy the phrases that Pignier dictated from the front of the room.

For the next few hours, the room hummed with conversation as the students debated the pros and cons of the new method. Some were enthusiastic about the dots while others objected to using anything other than letters. But even the skeptics could not deny that it was easier to feel the dots and dashes than the large, embossed letters of Haüy's books. Because it was faster, the students found that they were less likely to forget the beginning of a sentence by the time they reached the end. This greatly increased the amount of material that could be read at a single sitting, a quality Pignier found most satisfying.

The assembly finally adjourned and the students returned to their dormitories. That night, Louis lay on top of his cot and reviewed what he could remember in his head.

Something about Barbier's system felt right to him, and before he drifted off to sleep, he resolved to master it.

Because Pignier encouraged the use of sonography in the classroom, it was not difficult for Louis to find the time to practice it. But as the weeks passed, Louis became increasingly aware of several major flaws. First, sonography was too complicated. Barbier had based his system on a 12-dot cell (2 vertical columns of 6 dots each). Consequently, as many as 20 dots were needed per syllable and up to 100 for a single word. Louis believed that the sheer number of dots needed to represent each sound impeded the reader by making it difficult to remember the combinations. Second, because the combinations stood for sounds instead of letters, there were no provisions for spelling, punctuation, or numbers. Without these components, both reading and writing would be too restricted and would never provide the blind equal access to the world's knowledge.

Yet despite these flaws, Louis remained intrigued by the simplicity of the dots and dashes. Instead of becoming discouraged by the complexities and omissions of sonography, Louis set himself to the task of improving it. After Pignier granted his request to keep a slate and stylus in the dormitory, Louis used whatever free time he could find— during recess, between classes, and late at night—to experiment with the system.

When he felt that he had mastered the system as Barbier had developed it, he began to make modifications in its form and content. The teachers watched with some amusement as Louis sat day after day, hunched over his slate, punching away with the sharp, pointed stylus. Ironically, the very instrument that was to become his avenue to knowledge and independence was remarkably similar to the awl with which he had blinded himself at age three.

The more Louis worked with sonography, the more he became convinced that, with certain modifications, the dot system could be a communication breakthrough. And so, throughout the spring and into the summer of that year, he continued his experiments. Despite the increased effort required to concentrate on this project, his academic performance remained excellent.

When school was over, Louis returned home by stagecoach to Coupvray. His mother reacted to her son's thin, tired appearance by cooking him large, healthy meals and making sure that he slept well each night. Having ignored his health in favor of his work, Louis was glad for the respite that family life provided. By August, his cheeks were once again rosy and his energy had returned. Feeling fully rested, he resumed his experiments.

Long walks in the clean, fresh air of the countryside relaxed his body and readied his mind for creativity. Each day he returned rejuvenated from the surrounding hills and vineyards and, taking his customary seat on the front step of the workshop, punched dutifully away at dozens of sheets of heavy paper. Neighbors passing by assumed the 13-year-old had created his own solitary game in an effort to fend off loneliness. His family understood his intellectual intensity, however, and never questioned his endeavor. Although there were occasional remarks about Louis's "pinpricks," they were always made in the spirit of fun and curiosity.

When Louis returned to school in October, he felt that he had made enough progress in his work to warrant a presentation to the director. Dr. Pignier listened closely as Louis explained the modifications he had made in Barbier's system. Pignier was immediately impressed and offered to arrange a meeting between Louis and the captain. He believed that if the inventor and the school's brightest student collaborated, there would be even more progress made toward perfecting sonography.

There are no official records of the conversation that took place during the meeting between Barbier and Louis Braille. It is known, however, that Louis presented the captain with his ideas for adapting sonography to a more usable form for the blind. Major changes included reducing the total number of dots and dashes required, and making each combination stand for letters rather than sounds.

But the captain—far from being pleased that his invention had sparked further thinking on the part of a talented young pupil—was angry that Louis had suggested any changes at all. Not being blind himself, Barbier had little empathy for the realities of the day-to-day life of the visually impaired and therefore could not imagine why they would want a more comprehensive system than sonography.

The captain, like most sighted people of that day, had yet to shed his prejudice toward blind people. His reaction to Louis's ideas suggests that he shared the common belief that the blind were inherently less intelligent than the sighted. This biased attitude made it impossible for Barbier to conceive of a 13-year-old blind boy making any significant improvements to sonography. Highly insulted, he left the meeting in a foul mood, refusing to affirm or encourage Louis's efforts.

Once again, Louis felt frustrated and alone. The one man who knew the system as well as he did was not interested in helping him modify or improve it. It was up to Louis himself to decide how far the project should go—or if it should continue at all.

He reached a decision in less than a week. With or without help and support, Louis was determined to develop his own system of reading and writing. In his diary he wrote: "If my eyes will not tell me about men and events, ideas and doctrines, I must find another way. . . . If I cannot discover a way to read and write, to understand life about me and life from the past, then I shall kill myself."

Following his own creative instincts, Louis labored tirelessly over the next two years to complete the work he had begun before meeting with Barbier. Building on the two principal modifications that he had suggested to Barbier (reducing the number of dots and making each dot combination stand for a letter instead of a sound), Louis made additional revisions. He cut the number of dots needed per vertical row from six to three, thus reducing the total number of dots in each "cell" by half. He then numbered each dot (1-6) and eliminated the dashes completely.

Dividing the alphabet into thirds, Louis assigned various combinations of the top four dots to the letters *A* through *J*. He then added the bottom dot in the left-hand

This engraving, the frontispiece to Guillié's book, shows a teacher at the Royal Institute for Blind Youth teaching a student to write.

column (dot number three) to the first 10 combinations to form *K* through *T*. Dot number six was added to form *U* through *Z*. Because the letter *W* is not used in the French language, it did not exist in Louis's original alphabet. It was added later, however, to accommodate the English-speaking blind.

The radical changes that Louis imposed on sonography resulted in a method that was wholly different in form and content. Though Louis had been inspired by Barbier's dots, "braille"—as the system would come to be known—eliminated the complexities of sonography while providing its missing elements. The new system was as brilliant as it was simple. As author Gary Webster points out in *Journey into Light,* the fact that it was invented by a 15-year-old schoolboy was nothing short of miraculous.

[Braille's] achievement was of such startling nature and tremendous order that it can be compared only with those of men like Copernicus, Newton and Einstein. For in effect, he devised a new highway along which men can send their thoughts and dreams marching into the minds of other men.

The tablet used for writing braille contains grooves and slots that allow the writer to quickly line up the stylus and create impressions in the proper formations. Braille's system worked so well that he could write down anything read aloud to him and immediately read it back perfectly.

6

TEACHER, AUTHOR, MUSICIAN

IN THE FALL OF 1824, Louis demonstrated his system to Pignier. The director chose an article from the French newspaper *Moniteur* and slowly dictated the beginning paragraphs. Louis sat across from Pignier's desk and punched out the words with his stylus as the director read them out loud. "You can go faster," he informed the surprised director after a few lines. Pignier increased his pace until the whole article was completed.

Turning the paper over, Louis ran his fingers rapidly across the page and repeated the article verbatim. "Amazing! Simply amazing!" exclaimed the dumbfounded director. They repeated the process using examples of prose and poetry until Pignier was satisfied.

The director remained speechless, shaking his head in near disbelief. Louis's system was so efficient, so precise, so easily executed. From the moment he had met the blond-haired youth, Pignier had sensed that

Louis possessed a profound intelligence and a lively imagination. Yet, as he pondered the implications of the invention before him, Pignier realized that he had underestimated the boy's genius. At once, he called an assembly to introduce the system to the rest of the school.

Like the director, the students reacted with a mixture of delight and sincere admiration. Relieved of the burden of dozens of dots and dashes per word, the students quickly punched out sentences using just a few dots per line. They were excited to learn that by using only 6 dots, they could form 63 combinations. In addition, the new system included punctuation, accent marks (as important as the letters themselves in French), and numbers—elements that were lacking in Barbier's sonography.

The students eagerly discussed applications for the new method: taking notes, keeping a journal, writing letters home, or doing their own creative writing. Formerly, these could be done only with the help of a sighted person. Now, however, these and other skills could be mastered and carried out without assistance. Through the painstaking efforts of one of their fellow students, the door to intellectual independence was suddenly opened.

Based on the unanimous opinion of the students, Pignier suggested that Louis's system be adopted unofficially for classroom use. He instructed his staff to immediately modify Barbier's sonography equipment. By the end of the following week, the students were practicing on rulers with new sliding clips in which only six dots could be punched.

Realizing the broad implications of Louis's invention, Pignier requested that France's interior minister give it formal recognition as the official method of writing for the blind. He believed that government sanction was the first step in making the system available to blind people everywhere.

But the French government, still in a state of flux and uncertainty, was slow to act. The country had been in a

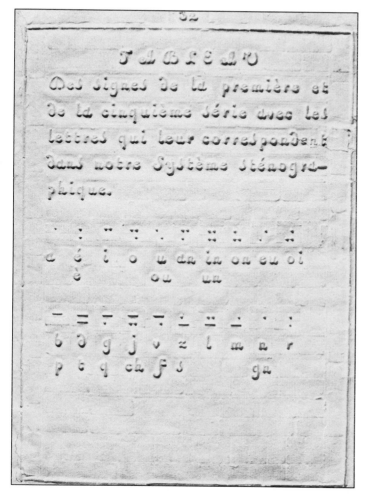

This early example of the braille alphabet used both dots and dashes. Further refinement of the system eliminated the dashes, yielding an alphabet composed of no more than six dots per letter.

constant state of upheaval since the Revolution of 1789, which had been followed by Napoléon's wars and endless power struggles and changes in the French government. The management of the Royal Institute for Blind Youth would itself be buffeted throughout Braille's life by the continual shifts in leadership between various Republican and Royalist forces at the national level. Pignier received congratulations for fostering Louis's work, but no mention of formal sanction was made. Pignier told Louis that he should not lose hope. In time, he said, the government would surely approve the new method.

Meanwhile, Louis's talents were expanding even further. In 1826, at the age of 17, he and his two closest friends—Gabriel Gauthier and Hippolyte Coltat—became apprentice teachers at the Institute. Leading classes in math, geography, grammar, and music, the three apprentices adhered to a philosophy that was based on mutual respect between teacher and student. They conducted their classes in an atmosphere of friendship and fun while maintaining high standards of academic achievement.

Unlike the other, sighted teachers, "Monsieur Braille" and his friends understood the feeling of vulnerability that accompanies blindness. Accordingly, they were careful to foster a sense of trust between themselves and their students. Punishments, if needed, were never harsh, and the teachers were especially understanding and gentle with the newest and youngest boys. The students—both

A chorus of blind students performs at the Institute. Music was one of the subjects that Braille taught as a professor at the Institute.

younger and older—found renewed interest in their lessons. In his booklet entitled "Historical Note on Louis Braille," Coltat wrote:

> The obligation of attending class was transformed into a real pleasure for his pupils . . . [who wanted] to please a teacher whom they admired as a superior and liked as a wise and well-informed friend.

After a two-year apprenticeship, Braille was made a full professor. Pignier, who had recognized Braille's aptitude from the start, offered him a private room with full board and a modest but adequate salary. In his new role as professor he would have the privilege of coming and going as he pleased. As long as he fulfilled his teaching obligations, there would be no more monitors, curfews, or limits imposed on Braille's leisure time.

At first Braille's schedule remained almost identical to the one he had followed as a student. Slowly, however, he began to enjoy his privacy and privileges. After he had finished lecturing for the day, he often joined Gauthier and Coltat for a long walk in the city's botanical gardens. In bad weather, they limited their strolls to the immediate neighborhood, stopping by their favorite pastry shop for some "petits gateaux chocolats" (chocolate cookies). During the quiet evening hours, Braille prepared lessons, wrote in his diary, and made further improvements in his dot system. He added musical notation and transcribed several of his favorite pieces of music.

At age 20, it seemed that Louis Braille had gained the independence and security that his parents had always hoped he would achieve. His position at the Institute gave him financial protection while providing him with a place to share his talents.

But Braille did not become complacent. His family heritage, small-community upbringing, and profound religious faith combined to fill him with a deep sense of commitment to others. For some, being a loyal and trust-

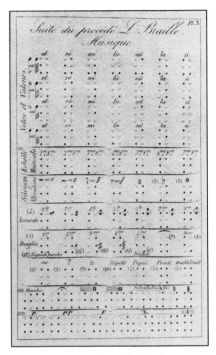

Braille, a gifted musician, adapted his dot system so that it could be used to record musical notation. Braille personally transcribed several of his favorite pieces of music to make them available to other blind musicians.

Braille's talent with the piano and organ was so great that he was hired as the official organist at one of the largest churches in Paris, St. Nicholas-des-Champs, pictured here.

worthy friend, an excellent musician, and a respected teacher would have been enough. But because Braille believed that his dot system could have significant, long-term impact on thousands of lives, he continued to concentrate his efforts on expanding and perfecting it.

Braille asked Pignier, who remained his strongest advocate, to renew his request to the government. "I will do all I can to help you," the director promised. But this time he warned Braille against getting his hopes too high. The French government was still undergoing changes as a result of both the Revolution and the former influence of Napoléon. In such unstable times, Pignier believed, it would be difficult to attract attention to the cause of the blind. Even if the issue was to be considered, consensus among the various political factions would be unlikely.

In 1829, Braille published a book explaining his "little system." The book, entitled *Method of Writing Words, Music and Plain Songs by Means of Dots, for Use by the*

Blind and Arranged for Them, marked the "formal birth" of Braille's method. In the preface, Braille gave full credit to Captain Barbier for introducing sonography to the Institute: "His method gave [me] the first idea," Braille wrote.

Throughout the 1830s, Braille continued to make small revisions in his basic dot alphabet. Concurrently, he increased the number of hours he spent practicing the piano and organ. Several local churches invited him to be a guest organist on Sundays, a request he was delighted to honor. Later, he was hired as the official organist at St. Nicholas-des-Champs, one of the largest churches in Paris. The position was a prestigious one and afforded Braille much respect from the musical community.

Parties at Pignier's home provided Braille with an additional forum for his music. The director made a point of inviting Braille, Coltat, and Gauthier to social gatherings so that the young men could meet people outside the Institute. As Braille's reputation as a fine musician grew, guests would ask him to perform their favorite pieces on the piano in Pignier's sitting room. Braille obliged them, but inevitably excused himself after a few numbers. He was uncomfortable being the center of attention, preferring to reserve his energies for worship rather than flaunt his abilities for entertainment.

In 1831, bad news reached Braille from Coupvray. On a warm May afternoon, Louis's brother Simon arrived to announce their father's passing. Braille cancelled classes for the rest of the week and returned to the village with Simon. The next day, Braille attended the funeral with his family. Nearly everyone in the village gathered around the wooden coffin to pay their last respects to their friend and fellow craftsman.

The event marked a low point in Braille's life. His father had been a warm, affectionate man, a good provider, and a strong believer in Louis's abilities. On his deathbed,

Simon-René had dictated a letter to Dr. Pignier asking him to never desert his son. Then, for additional security, he left the house and the farm in Louis's name.

Braille returned to the Institute still grieving but resolved, as always, to make his life count for something. He continued to work as hard as ever but maintained a good sense of humor and warmth of spirit. He drew courage

Paris's largest open square, La Place de la Concorde, is shown here in an 1890 photograph. At a major exhibition in the square in 1834, Louis Braille demonstrated his new, efficient system of reading and writing. Among the guests was King Louis Philippe, who was impressed but offered no official backing for Braille's method.

from his close friendships with Pignier, Gauthier, and Coltat, and his easy rapport with the younger students. Braille gained a reputation for lending money freely and rarely required reimbursement, especially from those who needed assistance with tuition. In his memoirs, Coltat later wrote: "[Louis] would have sacrificed everything for any one of us."

In 1834, an Exhibition of Industry was held on Place de la Concorde, the city's largest open square. Pignier, who continued to be frustrated in his requests to the Ministry of the Interior, saw this as the perfect opportunity to showcase Braille's work. Immediately, he registered Braille as an exhibitor.

By now, the dot alphabet was used almost exclusively at the Institute. (But because Haüy's method of embossed letters was still the "offical" system, it too was included in the curriculum.) To increase the use of the dot system, Braille transcribed more than a dozen books for classroom use. After years of daily practice, his writing was extremely fast and his reading speed approached 2,500 dots per minute.

At the Exhibition, Braille sat hunched over his slate for hours in a straight-backed chair, punching rapidly away with his stylus. Visitors read from books or dictated messages to him, and then watched with some curiosity as Braille copied the words into the dot alphabet. Their curiosity turned to admiration and surprise when the young blind professor, using his fingertips, read back each message exactly as it had been spoken.

Two of the visitors—King Louis Philippe and the minister of the interior—also witnessed Braille's exhibition. As they watched him taking rapid dictation, Braille hoped that his demonstration would convince them once and for all of the system's merit. Both the king and the minister asked questions regarding the process of Braille's invention and its practical uses. They flattered him with encouraging remarks and words of congratulations. Still, they gave no indication that there would be any action on the part of the government to designate Braille's method as the official one.

Braille left the Exhibition in much the same mood as he had left the meeting with Barbier 13 years earlier. He knew that without official sanction, his system was destined to remain an "auxiliary method" within the Institute.

Moreover, word of its existence might never spread much beyond Paris.

Plunging himself once again into his teaching and his music, Braille tried to forget the possibility that his system would exist only as long as he did. When he was not teaching or practicing the organ, he transcribed as much material as possible into the dot system. Thanks to his ambition, the Institute now had a sizable number of books and musical scores in its library.

But the long hours of work and the damp, ever-deteriorating conditions of the school building were beginning to take their toll. Like many of the students, Braille had developed a nagging cough that usually subsided after a few weeks of vacation in Coupvray. But in 1835, there were indications that his health was getting worse. Increasingly, he was overcome with fatigue, often suffered from fevers, and was plagued by a feeling of tightness in his chest. Pignier grew concerned and offered to lighten Braille's teaching responsibilities so that he could rest. After a particularly harsh bout of coughing accompanied by a high fever, Braille capitulated. The school physician was called in, and he made a quick but certain diagnosis: Louis Braille was suffering from tuberculosis, an incurable and deadly disease.

This portrait of Louis Braille was made from a daguerreotype, an early kind of photograph. Braille impressed all who met him not only with his obvious intelligence, but also with his humility and generosity.

7

THE DIFFICULT YEARS

IN THE MID-1800s, little was known about tuberculosis, or "consumption," as it was then called. It was not until 1882 that scientists were able to isolate the germ that caused this terrible and fatal disease. They also discovered that the germ flourished in damp, dirty, and overcrowded areas, a fact that helped to explain the prevalence of consumption cases at the Royal Institute for Blind Youth in Braille's time.

When Braille received the doctor's diagnosis in 1835, he accepted it without question. Nonetheless, he remained committed to carrying out his duties at the school and to continuing his improvements on the dot alphabet. He took some comfort in the fact that patients in the early stages of the disease nearly always showed some improvement if they rested, received plenty of fresh air, and paid proper attention to nutrition.

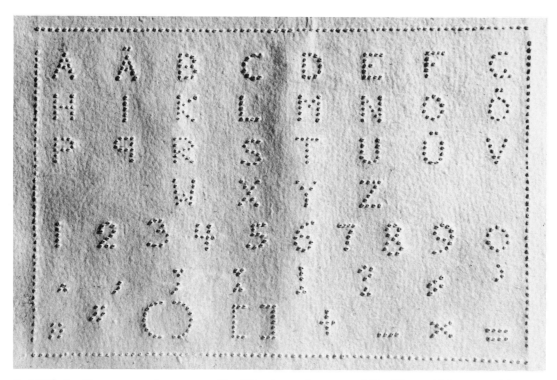

In 1839, Braille announced the invention of a new dot system that could be read by both blind and sighted people with no special training. In the new method, which was called raphigraphy, raised dots were arranged in the familiar shapes of the French alphabet, allowing blind students at the Institute to write letters to their sighted friends and relatives.

Dr. Pignier, who treated Braille as if he were his own son, was distraught upon hearing the prognosis. He immediately transferred Braille's classroom responsibilities to one of the other instructors, thereby limiting Braille's teaching obligations to just a few music lessons per week. Braille complied reluctantly with Pignier's restrictions, choosing instead to focus his diminishing energies on his own research.

In the weeks that followed, Braille spent hours in the nearby park, the school's courtyard, or alone in his room, resting and doing research. He gave a few music lessons, but these were short and did not require as much stamina and preparation as regular classroom teaching.

It was during this time that Braille completed a revised version of his first grammar book in which he explained in detail the rules and uses for his dot alphabet. In the course of his research, he began developing an idea for a new system, one that could be written by the blind, yet easily read by the sighted. Braille realized that in order for the method to be effective, it must combine the visual advantages of the sighted alphabet with the tactile advantages of raised dots.

In 1839, two years after finishing a revised version of his *Method* book, Braille announced the completion of his new writing system, which he called raphigraphy. Raphigraphy used raised dots to form the letters of the sighted alphabet as well as the various symbols of musical notation. It was less cumbersome than Haüy's embossed letters and, unlike the dot alphabet alone, did not require the sighted to learn a new language.

The students were jubilant when Braille presented them with his invention. For the first time they could write to sighted friends and relatives in a language anyone could understand. To facilitate the use of raphigraphy, Braille collaborated with a blind friend, François-Pierre Foucault, to create a printing method for it.

Together, they developed a machine that is considered the prototype of the modern typewriter. Large metal keys were fitted with the raised-dot letters of raphigraphy. When the keys were pressed down, they left an imprint that could be read with the eyes or felt with the fingertips. As a result, letters and other documents could be produced with far greater speed and efficiency than ever before.

Braille kept a raphigraphy machine in his room at the Institute, using it frequently to write to his mother in Coupvray. The following excerpt illustrates that despite periods of ill health and enforced rest, Braille maintained his optimism and his concern for the welfare of others:

> Please write to tell me if you are well and give me news of our relatives. . . . I was so pleased to hear that the weather had kept fine for the vintage. . . . But now . . . Winter has begun and one must stay indoors . . . let's keep smiling and get through [it].

Together with his friend François-Pierre Foucault, Braille invented a printing press that could type the raised letters used in raphigraphy. Their invention is considered the prototype of the modern typewriter.

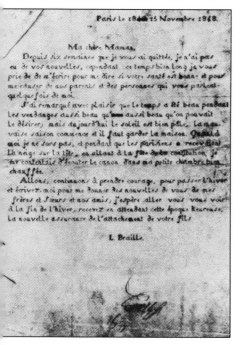

This letter, written in raphigraphy, was sent by Louis Braille to his mother in November 1848. Although Braille had been chronically ill for years, he maintained his cheerfulness, writing, "Winter has begun and one must stay indoors. . . . let's keep smiling and get through [it]."

Although his dot alphabet continued to be used in the classrooms at the Institute, it remained virtually unrecognized outside it. Pignier persisted in his attempts to petition government officials on Braille's behalf, but received no encouraging replies. Braille, sensing that time was short, sent letters and copies of his *Method* book to everyone he knew. Whenever he met someone who showed the slightest interest in his research, he would immediately oblige them with an impromptu demonstration of his "little system."

Wherever he was—in the park, at Pignier's home, or on the stagecoach to Coupvray—Braille spread the news of his invention with evangelistic zeal. Braille biographer Gary Webster wrote: "In spite of his illness and troubles, regardless of the world's indifference or active opposition, he intended both to live a good life and to leave behind a lasting gift to mankind. Though few took his ideas or discoveries seriously, he . . . clung to the notion that his system would one day enter universal use."

Dr. Pignier continued to be Braille's most enduring advocate. Yet despite the comfort he took in the director's unfailing patronage, Braille knew that there were teachers at the Institute who despised Pignier for his strong support of Braille's work. Because he was a soft-hearted administrator and held liberal political views, Pignier fell into further disfavor with his largely conservative staff.

In the spring of 1840, rumors circulated that Pignier would be asked to retire early. It was said that P. Armand Dufau—Braille's former geography teacher and Pignier's assistant—had conspired to have Pignier removed. Backed by testimony from several other instructors, Dufau convinced government officials that Pignier was "corrupting minds with his history teaching."

Had France's political system been in a more settled state, it is unlikely that Dufau's plan would have succeeded. But the French government had been vacillating between monarchy and democracy for the last quarter-century and was immediately suspicious of anyone—especially a government employee—who held liberal political views. Dufau capitalized on this fact, persuading the minister of the interior that Pignier should be fired.

Although he suspected that the minister's request had its origins within his own staff, Pignier left without bitterness. On a rainy Sunday morning of that same year, he left the front door of the Institute and "climbed into a waiting carriage, not turning his head to look back at the gray stone building where he had spent so many years," according to Braille biographer Anne Niemark.

Under Dufau, the mood of the school changed once again. The atmosphere became tense and conflict ridden, as it had been during Guillié's administration. Like Guillié, Dufau was quick to assert his authority, and he punished students severely for breaking the rules. He made rapid changes in scheduling, staff, and curriculum, seldom stopping to consider the needs or feelings of the students. In order to maintain complete control over both staff and students, Dufau made it clear that he would not tolerate teaching methods or ideas that conflicted with his own. He had opposed Braille's dot system from the beginning, maintaining that it gave the blind students too much independence. Instead, he preferred letters that he and the other sighted teachers could easily recognize, such as the ones used in Haüy's system. Dufau was also opposed to blind students becoming teachers. Like some of the other instructors at the Institute, he was afraid that the combination of a separate dot alphabet and access to professional positions would result in hundreds of sighted teachers, craftsmen, and musicians losing their jobs. His assumption was false, of course, but to a shortsighted, insecure man like Dufau, the threat seemed quite real.

Before Dufau took charge, Braille and Pignier had used the school's printing press to produce a multivolume history of France using the dot alphabet. Under Dufau, however, these books were confiscated in an attempt to discourage the students from learning Braille's method.

As the weeks passed and Dufau became more settled in his position as director, he became more aggressive in his persecution of the dot system. He banned its use in the classrooms and personally collected any slate or stylus he found in the dormitories. In place of the dot alphabet, Dufau advocated a smaller version of Haüy's embossed letters and ordered new books to be printed in this style. As the director waged his personal war against the dot alphabet, Braille's health declined further. His fatigue mounted, he lost weight, and his cough deepened. He often became breathless in the middle of a conversation and had to return to his room to rest. Fevers came more frequently, so he was forced to stay in bed for days or even weeks at a time.

As winter settled over the city in 1843, Braille's symptoms worsened. When his cough produced hemorrhaging (bleeding) in his lungs, the school's physician, Dr. Allibert, was called in. After making a thorough examination, Allibert informed the patient that his condition was critical. He recommended that Braille give up all of his teaching obligations and take an extended vacation in the country.

Feeling too weak to properly fulfill his duties at the Institute, Braille complied with the doctor's recommendation. His friend Gauthier immediately arranged for Braille's return to Coupvray.

The long ride in the hard-bouncing, drafty stage left Braille weak and overwhelmingly fatigued. Monique Braille, more anxious than ever about her son's health, was frightened by his pale, withered appearance. For the next few weeks she watched over him night and day, making sure that he ate the best food available and had complete quiet and rest. On the still, warm days, she sat with him in the bright sunshine at the kitchen window, feeding him herbal tea and simmering onion soup.

Among the teaching tools at the Royal Institute for Blind Youth was this globe, made for the school in 1833.

When he felt a bit stronger, Monique spread a quilt in the yard next to the house. Here, in the sunshine and fresh air, Braille rested quietly, reviving both his body and spirit with the familiar sounds and smells of the countryside. Each day, he faithfully ingested the sweet liquids in the small blue bottles that Dr. Allibert had prescribed. Each night, he drank several cups of tea that his mother made from the herbs she had purchased at the village market.

Gradually, the horrible cough subsided, the color returned to Braille's cheeks, and he began to gain weight. He took short walks around the property and sometimes ventured into the village itself.

By summer, Braille's condition had improved notice-
ably. His walks lengthened, occasionally taking him into
the surrounding hills and vineyards. He spent time each
day visiting old friends and neighbors and telling stories
to the children from the village school. Though not much
had changed in Coupvray since he had left for Paris in
1819, some of the most precious and important people in
Braille's life were missing. His former teacher Antoine
Becheret, his friend and mentor Abbé Palluy, and the
generous Marquise d'Orvilliers had all since died. Two
years earlier, Braille's older sister Marie-Céline had died
suddenly of a fever, leaving a son and a daughter behind.
Braille found that he enjoyed the company of his 15-year-
old nephew and 8-year-old niece, and he often invited them
on hikes through the countryside. As they walked, he made
a point of telling them the stories he had learned from
Marie-Céline when he was a boy.

Braille's steady physical recovery was accompanied by
intellectual restlessness. As soon as he could, he began
transcribing more books and musical compositions into
the dot alphabet. Sitting on a quilt in the sun next to
the cottage or perched on the step of the harness shop
(recently taken over by Catherine's two sons), he recom-
menced his life's work. This time, however, he was careful
to take frequent breaks and to enjoy being part of the
simple village life of Coupvray. "If you ever come to visit
me in Coupvray, I shall teach you how to milk a cow!" he
wrote in a letter to his friend Gauthier. To which Gauthier
promptly replied: "If you ever come to visit me at my home
in Paris, I shall allow you to sleep in a quilted feather bed!"

In the fall of 1843, Braille kissed his mother good-bye,
assuring her that her six months of constant care and
nursing had cured him for good. As he boarded the stage
for Paris, he felt stronger than he had in several years.

At the Institute, he was greeted warmly by Gauthier and
Coltat, and he immediately received an invitation to dine
at Pignier's home. But despite the goodwill of his friends,

Braille sensed that something was amiss. When he questioned his colleagues about the changes that had taken place during his absence, they were forced to tell him some bad news.

Dufau had seized the opportunity presented by Braille's absence to try to destroy the dot alphabet once and for all. Toward this end, he had ordered all of the books printed or transcribed in Braille's system to be burned in the school's courtyard. The students had no voice in the decision and could only stand by helplessly and listen to the crackling and popping of the book-fed bonfire. Then, much to their horror, dozens of slates and styli were added to the roaring blaze. "Sweep away this soot at once!" Dufau commanded the caretaker, as the last glowing ember was stamped out.

Braille reacted to the news of Dufau's treachery with disbelief. Though he had been aware of the director's opposition to the dot alphabet, he had not anticipated such a drastic and thorough attack. He felt confused and

A class of blind students studies at the Royal Institute for Blind Youth. Despite strict supervision, the students met secretly and continued to write in braille, even after the dot system was banned from the school. The youths collected pencils, forks, nails, and knitting needles, which they used to punch dots into paper.

AUX JEUNES-AVEUGLES. — Une classe.

Un voyant, moniteur.

defeated, but remained determined to keep his system alive in whatever way he could.

Fortunately, the students rallied in support of Braille. After all, it was he who had liberated their hearts and minds, and made them see their lives as valid and meaningful despite their visual handicap. They knew that if the dot alphabet were destroyed, any chance of their having an independent life would also be lost.

They began holding secret meetings in the dormitories to decide on a plan that would ensure the continuance of Braille's system at the Institute. They agreed that the younger students would discreetly collect pencils, forks, nails, knitting needles, or any object that was sharp enough to punch holes into paper. The older boys would find hiding places for these crude styli, collecting the needed paper from their sighted friends and relatives.

Despite the opposition of the conservative director of the Institute, P. Armand Dufau, the braille language would survive to spread to other continents. The book shown here, Aunt Sammy's Recipes for the Blind, was published by the U.S. Department of Agriculture.

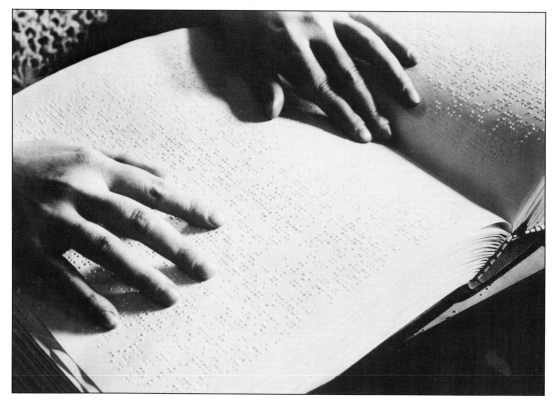

Armed with their makeshift tools, the older students taught the dot alphabet to the newer students. They sat up in the dormitory late at night, passed notes to each other in the halls between classes, and kept journals hidden underneath their beds. Some were caught and punished by being ordered into solitary confinement, sent to bed without dinner, or hit sharply across the back of their hands with a heavy ruler.

But Braille's determination in the face of adversity had inspired courage in the students as well. For the most part, they endured their punishments quietly and resumed their clandestine activities at the next available opportunity.

All but one of the sighted teachers at the Institute had supported Dufau's actions. Joseph Guadet, Dufau's personal assistant, watched with great interest as the battle over the dot system raged on. At first he did not discuss the issue with Dufau, preferring instead to remain a spectator to the "civil war" that his employer had instigated.

Gradually, however, it became clear that although the writing implements could be confiscated and the books burned to ashes, the concept of the dot alphabet was destined to remain alive in the hearts and minds of the students. Guadet had seen firsthand how the system had liberated the blind just as democracy was liberating the country. By the end of 1843, he could no longer remain silent on the issue. Privately and with the utmost discretion, he prepared to present his case to Dufau.

This diagram of the letters and numbers of the braille alphabet was printed in 1850 with the backing of M. Dufau, who had finally rescinded his opposition to the system.

8

THE STRUGGLE
ENDS

RECLINING IN THE PADDED leather chair in his office, Dufau listened carefully to his assistant's remarks. Guadet, in preparing to argue in favor of Braille's system, had taken his superior's obstinance and need for authority into consideration. Instead of trying to win Dufau over directly, Guadet wisely appealed to the director's ambitions.

He began by pointing out that Braille's method was the most efficient one ever invented. Consequently, more books and other printed material could be produced in the dot alphabet than in embossed letters. Guadet reasoned that the government would be more likely to allocate funds to produce these materials if more of them could be made in the same amount of time.

Second, because Braille's method surpassed all others in efficiency and ease of execution, it was sure to be recognized outside the Institute and put into universal use. Despite the administration's attempts to forbid its use, the students were determined to continue using it and to spread their knowledge to others. If Dufau did not claim credit for allowing the system to prosper, Guadet told him, then certainly someone else would.

After Guadet concluded his argument, the director remained silent and pensive for several minutes. Then he thanked Guadet for sharing his ideas and told him that he would take a few weeks to consider them further.

At the end of this period, Dufau acquiesced. He saw the logic in Guadet's thinking and—tired of fighting a losing battle with the students—lifted the ban on the dot alphabet. Both staff and students were now free to use it in the classrooms and dormitories.

The students rejoiced upon hearing the news. For Braille, who had resumed teaching upon returning from Coupvray, it was a particularly satisfying victory. The students would now have the opportunity to learn the method openly from its inventor rather than in secret or from a grammar book.

Though his health was not fully restored, Braille plunged enthusiastically into his duties. Dr. Allibert had told him that tuberculosis was an elusive disease, one that came and went for no apparent reason. Knowing that another attack of fevers and hemorrhaging could occur at

In 1843, the Institute was moved out of its dank, insanitary quarters into the glorious new facility pictured here. The cleaner, more spacious setting was not only more comfortable, but also healthier for the students and staff, many of whom, including Braille, had contracted tuberculosis in the old building.

any time, Braille was determined to make the best of each day.

Dufau's change of heart was a harbinger for more good news. In 1843, plans were being made to vacate the damp, run-down building on Rue St. Victor and to occupy a new one on the lovely Boulevard des Invalides. The new building, which was cleaner and more spacious than the old one, was ready in November of that year. As Braille and the other teachers helped prepare the students to move, they were filled with both anticipation and regret. Braille biographer Beverley Birch wrote:

> It must have been with a strange mixture of emotions that the pupils of Rue St. Victor packed up and moved. The insanitary old building had been home to many of them for years . . . ; perhaps Louis Braille would have never contracted tuberculosis had he spent his life . . . in healthful surroundings.

Escorted by members of the staff, the students were led down Rue St. Victor to their new home at 56 Boulevard des Invalides. Some of the boys cried as they left the front door of the old building for the last time. They knew they would miss the familiar sounds, smells, and textures of the place that most of them called home.

But there was excitement, too, at the prospect of more space, more bathrooms, and a cleaner, healthier environment. They would no longer have to sleep in one large room but would each share a smaller room with one or two classmates. Closets and dressers would be provided, and new uniforms had been ordered. These items were standard in sighted boarding schools, but they seemed like luxuries to the blind boys who had learned to live without such comforts.

Upon arriving at the new location, the boys listened eagerly as the sighted teachers described the building: "the brick arches over the windows, the sturdy turret on the roof, the tall iron fence with its two lanterns . . . the waving

The high, arching windows of the Institute's new building lent an air of luxury even to the girls' bathroom, shown here. Female students were admitted to the school for the first time in its 70-year history in 1844.

majesty of the French flag that jutted out from the front of the building." Inside, the boys were helped to find their rooms. On each carefully made bed there was a welcome gift from Dufau—a new writing slate designed to the specifications of Braille's dot alphabet.

After years of disappointment, Braille felt that at last he was making progress toward putting his system into universal use. There was still much to be done, but the first and most important step had been taken. Now, with the blessing of the school's director and the Institute's staff, Braille could continue his work with less worry and a lighter heart.

Dufau announced that the public dedication of the new school would take place in the auditorium the following February. There would be poetry readings, singing, a band performance, and a speech given by Dufau himself. Honored guests would include the students' friends and families, prominent citizens who had made private donations to the school, members of the board of directors, and several government officials.

During the next few months, both staff and students were busy preparing for the event. Invitations were drawn up and sent out, music was chosen, programs were printed, and the building was lavishly decorated. Eagerly, the students marked off the days and weeks on their calendars. As Dedication Day drew nearer, they could speak of almost nothing else.

February 22, 1844, dawned bright and sunny. The sunlight filtered through the windows of the auditorium, creating a natural spotlight on the stage. Student ushers distributed printed programs as the guests filled the rows of brightly colored, cushioned seats. The blind musicians, playing selections by famous composers such as Chopin and Gounod, sounded better and more confident than ever before.

When the musicians were finished, a hush fell over the crowded room. Dufau walked solemnly to the podium and began his speech. After extending a formal welcome to the guests on behalf of the staff and students, Dufau made an important announcement: a demonstration of Louis Braille's dot alphabet would be added to the program. Braille, who was seated in the front row beside Gauthier and Coltat, could hardly believe his ears. The director had given no hint that he intended to make such a presentation, yet in just a few moments, the public would be formally introduced to his work.

Dufau continued his speech, which included other important announcements. From now on, he explained, the Institute would be known as the National Institute for Blind Youth, a change that reflected the increasing influence of democracy in France. In addition, for the first time in its 70-year history, female students would be admitted to the Institute.

The speech was followed by hearty applause. When the clapping finally ceased, Dufau chose a volunteer from the audience and asked him to come up on the stage. At the same time, a young blind girl with long blond pigtails was led to a chair next to the podium. The director then asked the volunteer—a government official—to read out loud from a poetry book.

As the official recited, the girl took dictation using a slate and stylus. When the verse was complete, she turned over the paper and—reading the dots with her fingertips—repeated the poem exactly as it had been read.

The audience was astounded. Applause broke out immediately and lasted for more than five minutes. Many of the guests were aware of the internal struggle that had taken place over the use of the dot alphabet. This public demonstration was evidence of Dufau's commitment to support Braille's method and to promote it beyond the boundaries of the Institute.

Not everyone in the audience was easily convinced, however. Another government official challenged the authenticity of the demonstration by suggesting that the girl had previously memorized the poem. Luckily, Dufau had anticipated some skepticism and had thought of a way to quell any doubts. Politely, he asked the questioning official to read from something of his own choosing.

There are several versions of what happened next, but according to school legend, the official searched his pockets and found a ticket stub from a musical performance he had attended the previous week. With a nod from Dufau, he read out loud the name, date, time, and location of the performance.

As before, the blind girl punched the information into her paper and repeated each word without a single mistake. This time there could be no doubt—Braille's method was truly a breakthrough in the education of the blind. As the audience applauded, Dufau asked Braille to stand and be recognized for his invention. With shaking knees and a quiet smile, Braille rose and humbly acknowledged the applause.

On the evening following the dedication ceremonies, Braille walked alone in the church where he had first

The new building was officially inaugurated on February 22, 1844, with a ceremony accompanied by music and speeches. The ceremony included a public demonstration of Braille's raised-dot method before several government officials, marking the complete reversal of Director Dufau's opposition to the braille system.

learned to play the organ. In *Touch of Light,* Anne Niemark describes Braille's emotions at the time:

> Soberly, he knelt in the pew and offered his ardent thanks to God . . . the peace and silence of the church infused him with a feeling of great love and gratitude . . . his string of rosary beads was tightly gripped in his hands . . . the fingers that had wrought a miracle, reached up to touch the beads against his lowered eyelids. It was his 36th year, and he had not seen the sky, trees or grass since he had been a child of three. . . . But . . . he had found another way—for himself and others—to know the glory of such things.

Braille survived another bout of ill health during the first year at the new school. After he temporarily reduced his duties and got more rest, his cough subsided and his strength returned. In 1847, Dr. Allibert pronounced him well enough to resume teaching.

The next three years were relatively happy ones, and though Braille tired easily and endured a constant tightness in his chest, he was able to carry out his duties with enthusiasm.

In 1850, however, another attack of fevers and internal bleeding weakened him to the point of collapse. This time, he relinquished his teaching position for good. Dufau, who had gradually become more supportive, kept Braille on the payroll for the few music lessons he was able to give. In addition, he saw to it that Braille remained comfortable and received the best medical care possible.

The following year saw no improvement in Braille's condition. He spent more time in bed, transcribing books and musical scores into the dot alphabet. Never having indulged in self-pity, Braille remained more concerned about the welfare of his family, friends, and pupils than he was about himself. Using his own savings, he continued to provide scholarships for needy students. Likewise, he cancelled all debts from previous loans made to friends and students. "He never wanted to be thanked," wrote Dr.

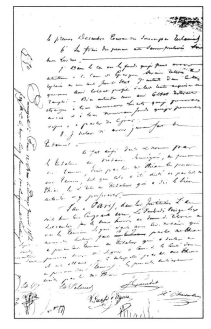

Louis Braille's will, shown here, ensured that his aging mother would be well provided for, and distributed the rest of his possessions among family and friends. Braille had long since canceled the debts of the many needy students whose tuitions he had paid out of his own pocket.

Louis Braille "never wanted to be thanked," wrote Dr. André Pignier, a one-time director of the Institute. Yet today, millions of blind people throughout the world share a limitless opportunity to read, write, and learn, thanks to the braille alphabet.

Pignier. His colleagues remarked that if Braille "had lived during the Middle Ages, he might have been canonized."

In mid-December, Braille experienced severe hemorrhaging of the lungs. He was admitted to the Institute's infirmary where he received round-the-clock care and was visited frequently by Coltat, Gauthier, and Pignier. They tried to cheer him by saying that he would soon be well again. But Braille knew better. "You don't have to pretend with me," he calmly told them. "I am convinced that my mission is finished on earth."

In preparation for the inevitable, he dictated his last will and testament. To his aging mother, he left a substantial annual income, and he divided the rest of his funds equally among his nieces and nephews. The land and buildings that his father had left to him Braille now left to his older brother Simon. Finally, he requested that all of his earthly possessions—music, books, instruments, clothing, and furniture—be divided among his closest friends.

On the morning of January 6, 1852, just two days after his 43rd birthday, the local priest delivered Holy Communion. Simon Braille had arrived from Coupvray and remained at his brother's bedside as the last spasms of coughing wracked Louis's feeble body. As the clock tower struck half past seven that evening, Louis Braille took his last breath.

The Paris newspapers made no mention of his death. Like many other great men and women whose contributions changed the course of history, Braille died virtually unrecognized and unknown. In the years to come, however, his work would open doors of opportunity to millions of blind people in countries all over the world. It is because of Louis Braille that the visually impaired have assumed their proper role—as learned, equal, and productive human beings—in contemporary society.

FURTHER READING

American Foundation for the Blind. *AFB Directory of Services for Blind and Visually Impaired Persons in the United States and Canada, 24th Edition.* New York, 1993.

———. *Louis Braille.* New York, 1990.

Birch, Beverley. *Louis Braille.* Milwaukee: Stevens, 1989.

Cole, Robert. *A Traveller's History of France.* New York: Interlink Books, 1992.

Davidson, Margaret. *Louis Braille: The Boy Who Invented Books for the Blind.* New York: Hastings House, 1972.

DeGering, Etta. *Seeing Fingers: The Story of Louis Braille.* New York: David McKay, 1962.

Keeler, Stephen. *Louis Braille.* New York: Bookright Press, 1986.

Keller, Helen. "Louis Braille: Light Bearer to the Blind." *Science Digest,* June 1952, 80–85.

Kettlecamp, Larry. *High Tech for the Handicapped.* Hillside, N.J.: Enslow, 1991.

Lende, Helga. "A Servant of Humanity." *Library Journal,* June 1952, 1027–33.

Niemark, Anne. *Touch of Light: The Story of Louis Braille.* New York: Harcourt, Brace & World, 1970.

"Precious Pods." *Time,* June 30, 1952, 42.

Roblin, Jean. *Louis Braille.* London: Royal National Institute for the Blind, 1960.

Swallow, Rose-Marie, and Kathleen Mary Huebner, eds. *How to Thrive, Not Just Survive.* New York: American Foundation for the Blind, 1987.

Webster, Gary. *Journey Into Light: The Story of Louis Braille.* New York: Hawthorn Books, 1964.

CHRONOLOGY

1809	Louis Braille born in Coupvray, France, on January 4
1812	Accidentally stabs himself in the eye with a sharp tool while playing in his father's harness shop; the wound becomes infected and the germs spread to his good eye, leaving Braille permanently blind
1815	Begins lessons with Abbé Palluy, the parish priest of Coupvray
1818	The Marquise d'Orvilliers writes to the Royal Institute for Blind Youth in Paris on Braille's behalf, asking that he be granted admittance
1819	On February 15, accompanied by his father, Braille leaves for the Paris school
1821	Dr. André Pignier replaces Dr. Sebastian Guillié as director of the Institute; Charles Barbier introduces sonography to the Institute
1822	Braille meets with Barbier to suggest improvements in his sonography system; Barbier is insulted and refuses to cooperate
1822–24	Braille invents a new alphabet, based on—yet radically different from—sonography
1824	Presents his system to Dr. Pignier and the students; the new alphabet is favorably received and is adopted unofficially for classroom use
1825	Pignier writes the first of many letters to the minister of the interior, requesting formal adoption of Braille's method
1826	Braille and two other blind students become apprentice teachers; Braille learns to play the organ
1828	Is promoted to full professor; he begins to develop a raised-dot system for music
1829	The first book explaining Braille's system is published; Barbier is credited for having inspired the use of dots
1831	Braille's father, Simon-René, dies
1833	Becomes the organist at St. Nicholas-des-Champs in Paris
1835	Is diagnosed as having tuberculosis
1835–36	Continues to give music lessons but reduces his classroom teaching; makes frequent visits to Coupvray in order to rest

1837	The Institute's printing press produces a multivolume history of France using Braille's raised-dot system
1838	After hearing testimony from doctors and concerned citizens regarding the dilapidated condition of the Institute, the French government allots money for a new building
1839	Braille invents raphigraphy, which combines the sighted alphabet with raised dots, allowing the blind to write to sighted people in a language both could easily understand
1840	P. Armand Dufau conspires against Pignier and takes over his position as director; Dufau bans the use of the raised-dot system at the Institute
1841	With his friend François-Pierre Foucault, Braille invents a raphigraphy machine, a prototype of the modern typewriter
1841–43	Reduces his teaching responsibilities because of ill health; returns to Coupvray to recuperate
1843	Braille's condition improves and he returns to Paris to resume teaching; learns that Dufau has destroyed all of the books that were printed in the raised-dot system
1844	Joseph Guadet persuades Dufau to lift the ban on the raised-dot system; when the new Institute building is opened, Dufau gives a public demonstration of "braille"
1846–47	Braille and Foucault develop the first braille printing press
1849–51	Braille's health declines rapidly and he is admitted to the Institute's infirmary
1852	Braille dies in Paris on January 6, just two days after his 43rd birthday; his body is taken to Coupvray for burial
1887	The citizens of Coupvray erect a statue in the town square in Braille's honor; Chemin des Buttes is renamed "Louis Braille Street"
1952	Braille's body is exhumed on June 30 and is transported to Paris for reburial in the Pantheon

INDEX

Alexander I (czar of Russia), 49

Allibert, Doctor, 92, 93, 101, 106

American Foundation for the Blind, 16

Barbier, Charles
 invents sonography, 62, 66
 offers sonography for use at Institute, 66–68
 rejects Braille's improvements upon sonography, 70–71, 84
 sonography modified by Braille, 69–73, 81

Becheret, Antoine, 42, 43, 44, 55, 94

Birch, Beverly, 101

Bonaparte, Napoléon, 28, 30, 37, 49, 77, 80

Braille, Catherine-Joséphine (sister), 22, 24, 25, 28, 34, 43, 51, 94

Braille, Louis
 accident leading to blindness, 17, 29–31, 34, 69
 adjustment to blindness, 34–41
 birth, 13, 21, 22
 childhood, 16, 17, 23–45, 69
 death, 18, 107
 education, 15, 17, 40, 41, 42, 43, 44, 45, 50–70
 ill health 85, 87, 89, 92, 93, 101, 106, 107
 intellect, 13, 17, 27, 40, 41, 42, 57, 70

internment and reburial in the Pantheon, 13–19
 meets Charles Barbier, 71
 musical abilities, 17, 56, 79, 80, 81, 85, 88, 106
 publications, 80, 81, 88, 89, 90, 101
 invents raised-dot alphabet, 70–75
 invents raphigraphy, 89
 religious faith, 40, 41, 79, 81, 105, 106
 teaching, 78, 79, 80, 85, 87, 88, 92, 100

Braille, Louis-Simon (brother), 22, 24, 25, 51, 81, 107

Braille, Marie-Céline (sister), 22, 24, 25, 28, 51, 94

Braille, Monique Barron (mother), 17, 21, 22, 24, 25, 26, 28, 30, 31, 34, 35, 37, 38, 39, 40, 43, 44, 45, 51, 54, 70, 89, 92, 93, 107

Braille, Simon-René (father), 17, 21, 22, 23, 25, 26, 27, 28, 30, 31, 34, 37, 38, 39, 40, 43, 44, 45, 50, 51, 52, 81, 82

Coltat, Hippolyte, 78, 79, 81, 83, 94, 103, 106

Consumption. *See* Tuberculosis

Coupvray, France, 13, 15, 17, 21, 24, 26, 27, 28, 34, 37, 40, 42, 51, 52, 55, 66, 70, 81, 85, 89, 90, 92, 94, 100, 107

D'Orvilliers, Marquise, 44, 45, 94

Dufau, P. Armand
 assumes directorship of Institute, 91
 bans use of raised-dot alphabet, 91–92, 95, 96
 conspires against André Pignier, 90–91
 strict teaching methods of, 52, 53, 54, 58
 withdraws opposition to Braille's system, 99–106

Einstein, Albert, 73

Exhibition of Industry, Paris, 84

Foucault, François-Pierre, 89

French Academy, 49

Gauthier, Gabriel, 53, 54, 56, 68, 78, 79, 81, 83, 92, 94, 103, 106

Guadet, Joseph, 97, 99, 100

Guillié, Sebastien, 49, 50, 52, 54, 58, 63, 64, 91

Gutenberg, Johannes, 13, 15

Haüy, Valentin
 embossed-letter alphabet of, 49, 58–61, 68, 84, 89, 91, 92, 99
 founds Royal Institute for Blind Youth, 49
 goes into exile for liberal views, 49, 50
 pioneers education for the blind, 47–50

returns to Institute and meets Braille, 64–66
"Historical Note on Louis Braille" (Coltat), 79

Journey into Light (Webster), 73

Keller, Helen, 15, 17, 19

Lende, Helga, 16
Lesueur, François, 48, 49
Louis XVI (king of France), 49
Louis XVIII (king of France), 37, 66
Louis Philippe (king of France), 84

Method of Writing Words, Music and Plain Songs by Means of Dots, for Use by the Blind and Arranged for Them, 80–81, 88, 89, 90, 101

National Institute for Blind Youth, 15, 103, 104, 105, 106. *See also* Royal Institute for Blind Youth
Niemark, Anne, 34, 91, 105

Palluy, Jacques, 40, 41, 42, 43, 44, 45, 55, 94
Pantheon, the, 15, 16
Paris, France, 14, 15, 17, 27, 37, 42, 44, 45, 49, 50, 51, 85, 94
Pignier, André, 52, 56, 63, 64, 67, 68, 69, 70, 75, 76, 77, 79, 80, 82, 83, 84, 88, 90, 91, 94, 106
Prejudice against the blind, 17, 33, 34, 47, 48, 49, 71

Raised-dot alphabet, 13, 15, 17, 18, 19, 80, 81, 88, 89, 90, 91, 101, 102, 103, 106
difficulty gaining governmental support for, 76–77, 84
invention of, 70–75
public demonstrations of, 75, 84, 104, 105
suppression of, 92, 95, 96, 97, 99, 100, 104

Raphigraphy, 89, 90
Raphigraphy machine, 89
Revolution of 1789, 49, 50, 77, 80
Roblin, Jean, 23
Royal Institute for Blind Youth, 17, 45, 47–55, 56, 57, 58, 60, 61, 63–64, 65, 66, 67, 77, 79, 81, 82, 83, 87, 89, 90, 92, 94, 96, 99, 101, 102, 103. *See also* National Institute for Blind Youth

Sonography, 66, 67, 68, 69, 70, 71, 73, 75, 81

Touch of Light (Niemark), 34, 105
Tuberculosis, 85, 87, 101, 107

United Nations Education, Scientific and Cultural Organization (UNESCO), 19

Webster, Gary, 13, 49, 61, 73, 90

PICTURE CREDITS

André Allibe/Musée Louis Braille: p. 29; Maria-Vincenza Aloisi: p. 36; Courtesy American Foundation for the Blind: pp. 14, 56, 59, 60, 61, 72, 74, 79, 98; Archives Jean Roblin/Musée Louis Braille: pp. 22–23; Bettmann: pp. 32, 37, 38–39, 65, 82–83, 89, 96; Bibliothèque Nationale, Paris: pp. 41, 50, 78, 80, 95, 100, 104; Jean Loup Charmet, Paris: pp. 46, 48, 77, 88, 93, 102; Harlingue-Viollet, Paris: pp. 2, 107; from *Histoire Populaire de la France,* by Duruy: p. 106; Musée Louis Braille: pp. 20, 55, 62, 86, 90; © Photo R. M. N./Louvre: p. 44; Photo by Jean Roblin: p. 67; Roger-Viollet, Paris: p. 25; UPI/Bettmann: pp. 12, 16, 18.

Jennifer Fisher Bryant is a freelance writer who specializes in biographies and has written 11 books, including *Marjory Stoneman Douglas: Voice of the Everglades* and a 75-page compilation of nature quotations. A former high school teacher of French and German, Bryant holds a bachelor of arts degree in French and Secondary Education from Gettysburg College. She lives in Glenmoore, Pennsylvania, with her husband and daughter.

ACKNOWLEDGMENT
The author dedicates this book to Ron Martorella, who made a lasting impression.

Jerry Lewis is the National Chairman of the Muscular Dystrophy Association (MDA) and host of the MDA Labor Day Telethon. An internationally acclaimed comedian, Lewis began his entertainment career in New York and then performed in a comedy team with singer and actor Dean Martin from 1946 to 1956. Lewis has appeared in many films—including *The Delicate Delinquent, Rock a Bye Baby, The Bellboy, Cinderfella, The Nutty Professor, The Disorderly Orderly,* and *The King of Comedy*—and his comedy performances continue to delight audiences around the world.

John Callahan is a nationally syndicated cartoonist and the author of an illustrated autobiography, *Don't Worry, He Won't Get Far on Foot.* He has also produced three cartoon collections: *Do Not Disturb Any Further, Digesting the Child Within,* and *Do What He Says! He's Crazy!!!* He has recently been the subject of feature articles in the *New York Times Magazine,* the *Los Angeles Times Magazine,* and the Cleveland *Plain Dealer,* and has been profiled on "60 Minutes." Callahan resides in Portland, Oregon.